ASIA and EUROPE

**Essays and Speeches
by
Tommy Koh**

ASIA and EUROPE

Essays and Speeches by Tommy Koh

edited by

Yeo Lay Hwee
Asad Latif

ASIA-EUROPE
FOUNDATION

World Scientific

Published by
World Scientific Publishing Co. Pte. Ltd.
P O Box 128, Farrer Road, Singapore 912805
USA office: Suite 1B, 1060 Main Street, River Edge, NJ 07661
UK office: 57 Shelton Street, Covent Garden, London WC2H 9HE

British Library Cataloguing-in-Publication Data
A catalogue record for this book is available from the British Library.

Published in collaboration with

Asia-Europe Foundation
No. 1 Nassim Hill
Singapore 258466
www.asef.org

ASIA AND EUROPE
Essays and Speeches by Tommy Koh

Copyright © 2000 by the Asia-Europe Foundation

ISBN 981-02-4412-6 (pbk)

Printed in Singapore

Dedication

*I would like to dedicate this book
to all the governors and colleagues at ASEF*

Tommy

ASEF Governors

Amb Dr Wolfgang Schallenberg (Austria), Amb Eric Duchene (Belgium), Dato Paduka Haji Suyoi Haji Osman (Brunei), Mr Liu Jieyi (China), Amb Jørgen Ørstrøm Møller (Denmark), HE Mr Olli-Pekka Heinonen (Finland), Mr François Xavier Ortoli (France), Professor Dr Helmut Haussmann (Germany), Amb Sotirios Mousouris (Greece), Professor Dr Edi Sedyawati (Indonesia), Amb Koji Watanabe (Japan), Amb Jay-Hee Oh (Korea), Mr Edmond Israel (Luxembourg), Dr Ghulam-Sarwar Yousof (Malaysia), Amb Roland van den Berg (the Netherlands), Amb Luz del Mundo (the Philippines), Dr Carlos Monjardino (Portugal), Mr J Y Pillay (Singapore), Amb Camilo Barcia (Spain), Mr Erland Ringborg (Sweden), Amb Vitthya Vejjajiva (Thailand), Sir Timothy Lankester (United Kingdom), Amb Do Cong Minh (Vietnam), and Dr Horst Krenzler (European Commission)

Former ASEF Governors

Amb Patrick van Haute (Belgium), Dato Haji Ahmad Matnor & Pengiran Hajjah Masrainah Pengiran Haji Ahmad (Brunei), Mr Zhang Yishan & Madam Zhang Xiaokang (China), Amb Niels Kaas Dyrlund (Denmark), Professor Dr Fuad Hassan (Indonesia), The late Amb Sean Ronan (Ireland), Professor Adriano Rossi (Italy), Mr Lee Sang-Ock (Korea), Datuk Emam Mohd Haniff

& Datuk Zakiah Hanum binti Abdul Hamid (Malaysia), Dr Yeo Ning Hong (Singapore), Mr Enrique Fanjul (Spain), Amb Finn Bergstrand (Sweden), Mr Tran Quang Co & Amb Dao Huy Ngoc (Vietnam)

ASEF Colleagues

Pierre Barroux, Duncan Jackman, Ulrich Niemann, Cai Rongsheng, Peggy Kek, Terence Tan, Jenny Fong, Andreas Sieren, Amelia Lim, Sharon Ong, Geraldine Ang, Marie Le Sourd, Carolyn Byrne, Yap Su-Yin, Jenny Tan, R Maggie, Christine Sipiere, Betty Ng, Angie Toh, Tia Siew Keng, Wendy Lee, Satwant Kaur, Velu, and Basri

Former ASEF Colleagues

Lee Geok Lian and Leigh Pasqual

Contents

Dedication	v
Foreword by Ambassador Jay-Hee Oh	ix
Foreword by Edmond Israel	xi
Acronyms	xiii
Introduction by Asad Latif	xv

Asia and Europe in an Emerging New World Order

The Asia–Europe Summit: A Journey of Rediscovery	3
East Asia, Western Europe and North America: A New Trinity in International Relations	7
Asia's Future and Its Relations with the West	13

Building Bridges: Business Ties, Cultural Exchange and Intellectual Dialogue

Building Bridges among the Young: The Message from Miyazaki	23
Towards a Productive Asia–Europe Business Relations	28
Towards a Common Economic Agenda in the Post-Crisis Era	33
The Importance of Cultural Exchange and Cooperation between Asia and Europe	36
The Importance of Cultural Development	41

Towards a Constructive Dialogue on Human Rights 45
Asian Values Reconsidered 50
What Can East Asia Learn from the European Union? 59

**Crisis and Change within Asia and Europe:
  Implications for Asia–Europe Relations**

The Second Asia–Europe Rendezvous in London 67
The East Asian Economic Crisis: Lessons Learnt and
  Prospects for Recovery 72
Is ASEAN Dead or Alive? 84
Beyond the Clouds 90
Asia's Stake in the Euro 94
The Euro: Separating Fact from Fiction 97

A New Asia and a New Europe

Europe and East Asia Need to Get Acquainted 107
East Asia in the 21st Century 110
Singapore: A New Venice of the 21st Century 116
The Nordic Community: A View from East Asia 120

The Bridge-Builder: The Asia–Europe Foundation

Report Card on the Asia–Europe Foundation 129
ASEF: Enhancing Mutual Understanding between
  Asia and Europe 132
The ASEF Story: The First Three Years 137

Foreword

Jay-Hee Oh
ASEF Governor for Korea
Chairman, ASEF Board of Governors

The year 1996 marked a watershed in the relationship between Asia and Europe. The first Asia–Europe Meeting (ASEM) was launched in Bangkok in March 1996, with the participation of 26 leaders, 10 from Asia, 16 from the EU. It was a historic event aimed at establishing a balance among the three major poles of the political and economic spheres — North America, Asia and Europe — by strengthening the weak link between the two regions of Asia and Europe.

ASEM, which was initiated by Prime Minister Goh Chok Tong of Singapore, held its second meeting in April 1998 in London. The next meeting will be held in October in Seoul this year.

Among the decisions taken at ASEM I in 1996 was the adoption of Singapore's proposal to establish the Asia–Europe Foundation (ASEF). This was exceptional since ASEM had vowed to avoid institutionalisation of the ASEM process. Establishment of the Foundation therefore is a manifestation of the importance the leaders attach to enhancing understanding and exchanges between the peoples of Asia and Europe. ASEF was subsequently founded in February 1997 in Singapore with the mission of promoting intellectual, cultural and people-to-people exchanges.

The challenge faced by ASEF in implementing the instructions of ASEM leaders was daunting, to say the least. It fell upon

Professor Tommy Koh to take up this challenge as ASEF's first Executive Director.

Professor Koh, Singapore's former ambassador to the United Nations and to the United States of America, successfully rose to the challenge with skill, creativity and passion. His dual background as both a seasoned diplomat and an accomplished scholar proved to be an invaluable asset.

Under his able leadership ASEF has developed within a short time into a prestigious institution. More than fifty high-quality projects have been conceived, planned and implemented under the auspices of ASEF. ASEF's achievements, which were presented by Professor Koh at the second Asia–Europe Meeting in London, received support and recognition from ASEM leaders.

The ASEF Board of Governors met in Vienna in May 2000. They decided that, at ASEM III in October this year in Seoul, the Board would report to the leaders on the progress made in ASEF's activities and propose financial plans and other ways to expand the work of ASEF. The Asia–Europe Vision Group, which was initiated by the Korean Government, recommended the expansion and strengthening of ASEF's work in its report to ASEM III.

This volume bears witness to the efforts, commitment, creativity, passion and wisdom of Professor Koh. It also showcases ASEF's rich accomplishments and is an important documentary of ASEF's contributions to the advancement of the ASEM process.

Professor Tommy Koh completes his term as ASEF's Executive Director at the end of October 2000. The mark he has left on ASEF and the ASEM process, however, will last for generations to come.

Foreword

Edmond Israel
ASEF Governor for Luxembourg
Past Chairman, ASEF Board of Governors

Through his lectures and his writings Professor Tommy Koh holds a fascination for the people who read and hear him. And these people come from a wide range of society, from many different parts of the world.

This is because while Ambassador Tommy Koh is rooted in the culture of Asia where he was born, his thinking is borderless. It crosses the boundaries of civilisations and cultures. He is a man of the 21st century and represents New Thinking for a New Century.

For me personally, it has been a gratifying experience to know Tommy, to become his friend and to work with him at ASEF. ASEF carries quite distinctly the imprint of his personality and of his thinking He has held the position of Executive Director of ASEF since its inception in February 1997. In the last three years, Tommy, a thinker and doer, has led the institution to implement nearly 60 major projects in its mission statement to promote engagement between the civil societies of Asia and Europe and to forge mutual understanding between the two regions.

We are grateful to Tommy for these achievements. At the same time I want to express my appreciation to those who have taken the initiative in publishing his writings. Tommy's essays and speeches reflect his personal conviction of the need to create bonds of understanding and friendship between the peoples of Asia and Europe, so that Asians and Europeans may be prepared to address the challenges and grasp the opportunities of this common world of ours.

Dear Tommy, we wish you well. We are also confident that in the future we can continue to count on your support. We know that you will continue relentlessly to communicate to the world your message, a message of peace and tolerance that invites all of us to build a better world for our generation and the generations to come.

Acronyms

AEBF	Asia–Europe Business Forum
AFTA	ASEAN Free Trade Area
ARF	ASEAN Regional Forum
ASEAN	Association of Southeast Asian Nations
ASEF	Asia–Europe Foundation
ASEM	Asia–Europe Meeting
APEC	Asia–Pacific Economic Cooperation
EALAF	East Asia–Latin America Forum
ECB	European Central Bank
ESCB	European System of Central Banks
EEC	European Economic Community
EMU	European Monetary Union
EU	European Union
EURATOM	European Atomic Energy Community
FDI	Foreign Direct Investment
GDP	Gross Domestic Product
GNP	Gross National Product
IMF	International Monetary Fund
MBA	Master of Business Administration

NAFTA	North American Free Trade Agreement
NATO	North Atlantic Treaty Organisation
NGO	Non-Governmental Organisation
NIEs	Newly Industralising Economies
ODA	Official Development Assistance
OECD	Organisation for Economic Cooperation and Development
OSCE	Organisation for Security and Cooperation in Europe
PLO	Palestine Liberation Organisation
SOM	Senior Officials Meeting
UNDP	United Nations Development Programme
WTO	World Trade Organisation

Introduction

Asad Latif

Asia played an ancient role in the making of Europe. Europa was an Asian princess whose abduction by the Greek god Zeus, disguised as a white bull, is said to have formed the basis of the continent that bears her name today. Since those mythological times, Asia's contribution to Europe has undergone many transformations. Sadly, they include Asia having turned into Europe's Other.

The transformations preceded colonialism, but led on directly to it. "Asia suffers, yet in its suffering, it threatens Europe: the eternal, bristling frontier endures between East and West, almost unchanged since classical antiquity," Edward Said wrote in his classic book, *Orientalism*. Today, it is colonialism that provides the most formidable legacy of Europe's role in the shaping of Asia. From ideas to institutions, from language to law, and from values to venison, the realities of post-colonial Asia bear the enduring stamp of Europe. Attempts to recover Asia's authentic pre-colonial past by erasing the European intrusion have not succeeded, no matter how sincere and fervent they have been. Europe arrived as the quintessential Outsider, but stayed on to become the inexhaustible Insider. It became an ineradicable part of Asia's past.

There was a twist to that story after the Second World War. The rise of the United States, the challenge from the Soviet Union, and the Cold War eclipsed Europe in the process of dividing it into two camps. Decolonised Asia fared worse. Korea,

Vietnam and Afghanistan became sites for the contending imperiums of Washington and Moscow, deadly terrains where Asians were forced to choose between the capitalist and socialist versions of peace, justice and utopia. Europe watched listlessly from the sidelines of history.

The fall of the Berlin Wall and the downfall of the Soviet Union initiated the phase of history which the world inhabits today. Interestingly, even as the defeat of the socialist alternative attested to America's supremacy in the Cold War, it presaged the arrival of a world in which the reunification of Europe would redraw the boundaries of international relations. In Asia, that other theatre of superpower engagement, the denouement would not be as dramatic, but the region, too, resumed a journey that had been interrupted by the forced march of the Cold War.

In the aftermath of that march, which turned out to be a detour after all, Europe and Asia found a new freedom to walk together, if they so pleased. Finally, after hundreds of divisive years, the two continents could look towards the single destination of equality.

A pleasant step was taken in 1996, when a proposal by Singapore Prime Minister Goh Chok Tong launched the Asia–Europe Meeting (ASEM) to chart the widening contours of the intercontinental relationship. The Singapore-based Asia–Europe Foundation (ASEF) appeared the following year as the most concrete result of that new-found engagement.

Professor Tommy Koh is something of an enigma. He is one of Singapore's foremost "Americans": he served as its hugely successful ambassador to Washington. When he turned "European" on being appointed director of ASEF, it appeared, even to his many admirers, that his new job indicated little more than the logic of diplomatic turnovers. A successful ambassador to the North Pole should be able to function equally well in the South Pole, and anywhere in between.

But Professor Koh, also an Ambassador-at-Large, took his Atlantic job to heart with the same quixotic seriousness that had defined his Pacific foray. His job was quixotic in an inverted sense. Good envoys would not be required were relations between countries and continents to be good: They are necessary precisely because realities, tilting one way or the other, are never balanced to make relations good enough. A good diplomat does not tilt at windmills: he tries to ensure that windmills are not built on tilted ground.

As Asia and Europe initiated a new phase in their relations, there was a need for someone who could bridge the two sides by being rooted enough in one to reach out meaningfully to the other. Professor Koh took on the job.

The lectures in this book reveal how this intellectual, part nomad and part pilgrim, crossed boundaries because, being a citizen of the world, he is contained nowhere and rooted everywhere.

His speeches span the three crucial areas of economics, politics and culture.

Economics

On economics, he notes in one of his lectures that ASEM "is not and should not be viewed as being at the expense of Europe's transatlantic ties or East Asia's transpacific ties". Rather, ASEM is the third side of the triangle linking the three centres of the global economy: North America, Western Europe and East Asia. That said, it is easy to forget, as he observes elsewhere, that although the US economy accounts for 25 per cent of the world economy, the European Union (EU) actually contributes more: 29 per cent. As for East Asia, its share of the global economy grew from a mere 9 per cent in 1965, to 15 per cent in 1975, to 24 per cent in 1993, and to 25 per cent in 1996, the year before the Asian economic crisis struck. That growth gave Europe an expanding stake in the region. Thus, in 1996, the EU exported US$123 billion of goods and services to East Asia, more than even the US. These facts make the "huge knowledge gap" between Asians and Europeans all the more lamentable, although the gap can be explained partly by America's looming profile in contemporary affairs. The Asian crisis, terrible though it was for the countries affected, had one silver lining, however: It reiterated the need for Europe to remain engaged economically in the region. Indeed, Europe's contribution to Asia's recovery was substantial and, commendably, it prevented protectionist forces at home from hijacking the international agenda.

Professor Koh examines these issues and others, such as the lessons of the EU for Asian integration, and the euro's implications for the global balance of economic power and hence Asia's own prospects in the new era. His overall concern is to underscore what both regions must do, in partnership with the US, to first sustain and then increase the momentum towards globalisation in the direction set by the World Trade Organisation. There will be obstacles to trade and investment liberalisation, he acknowledges frankly, but there is no alternative to the process, he says, equally bluntly.

Politics

Does East Asia, home to the successful 10-member Association of Southeast Asian Nations (ASEAN), have the political will to take cooperation a step further and realise the vision of an East Asian Community? Asia's remarkable economic growth and social development were fostered in part by increased intra-regional trade and investment, which gave rise to the need for more consultation and dialogue. The 1997–1998 crisis slowed down that process, but it has also the beneficial result of showing East Asians "the desirability of uniting the region and building new institutions to serve the region". Professor Koh does not deny the diversity of historical experience and current conditions that prevents East Asia from attaining the degree of integration seen in Europe now. But he hopes (and this is the hope of a thinker well-versed in the sobering realities of international affairs) that an East Asian Community is not a pipe dream. After all, what the EU is today began as the European Economic Community. And where economics leads, politics has little choice but to follow. The trend towards an East Asian Community, muted though it is now, forms one of the underlying themes of the essays in this book.

Another political theme is the disagreement between Europeans and Asians over human rights and democracy. Professor Koh does not fudge the difference by settling for a fictitious universalism that denies the divergent historical and political trajectories of the two continents. Neither does he conclude that the twain shall never meet. What he does is to show why and how Europeans and Asians can work towards the bridging of a real divide by seeking to learn from each other's perspectives and perceptions. Learning is a far more worthwhile effort than the easy denunciation that takes the form of attributing motives to and casting aspersions on the other side's arguments and dismissing them as self-serving. Whether or not readers are convinced by what he says, his work as an intellectual peacemaker, building on the realisable foundations of empirical evidence, is undeniable. Astringent but not acerbic, pointed but not pugnacious, that role is one which more Tommy Kohs should be shouldering. In that context, what stands out is his ability to hold a mirror to both Europe's and Asia's views of each other even as he remains a Singapore official and interlocutor. That ability is, perhaps, the advantage which a scholar-diplomat enjoys. He seeks to base the necessary compromises of diplomacy on the dispassionate intellectual rigour which scholarship enjoins on its devotees.

Culture

Professor Koh's devotion to culture provides yet another strand of these lectures. It is a defining and sustaining strand. Man does not live by bread and rice alone, as he says; neither can even politicians politick all the time. Humans need culture to be themselves. So do Asians and Europeans, inheritors of two ancient civilisations. It is culture that makes them what they are today. With a keen, instinctive feel for the agency of culture in the making of secure individuals and societies, he suggests how its resources, both traditional and evolving, can act as a catalyst in healthy and balanced interactions between Europe and Asia. He has no patience for philistines, but he also gives no quarter to culture vultures which fly in others' borrowed skies. In one of his lectures on culture, he confesses that he feels like a mosquito in a nudist camp: "I know what I am supposed to do but I am not sure where to begin." That jocular exercise in modesty is belied by his exploration of how the arts and culture can use the possibilities created by the international market in ideas to create networks between Asia and Europe. Their exchange should take three forms, he says: the exchange of finished products; the exchange of techniques or forms; and the sharing of the creative process. He calls for an index ranking countries by the quality of life, an index that would include cultural (and environmental) indicators in addition to economic and social factors.

After the conclusion of a major international conference in Singapore, a participant asked: What is the difference between a journalist and a diplomat? He gave an answer. A journalist is a person who bursts into a press conference and accosts a diplomat with the question: "Didn't you just say that woman has a face which would stop the hands of a clock?" A diplomat is a person who replies without batting an eyelid: "No, I said that when I look into her eyes, time comes to a standstill."

As the audience roared with laughter, the speaker noted that the target of his compliment was the consummate diplomat, Tommy Koh. There are no ugly women and men in this book. There are only humans, some ordinary and others extraordinary, and the continents they inhabit. Professor Koh's success lies in the extraordinariness with which he invests their everyday lives. He says that even while Europeans and Asians go about being themselves, day after anonymous day, they are building something precious.

It is a sustainable world. That world is not exclusively Asian or European. It belongs to all.

ASIA AND EUROPE IN AN EMERGING NEW WORLD ORDER

Asia's historical encounter with Europe provides the backdrop to the transformation which their engagement is undergoing today. Their relations are pivotal in world affairs, whose other nexus is North America. The essays in this section examine various facets of the intercontinental relationship.

The Asia–Europe Summit
A Journey of Rediscovery

The Three Encounters

Europe's encounter with Asia can be divided into three historical phases.

In the year 1271, Marco Polo of Venice made his historic journey to China. He returned to Venice in 1295 and published his book, *Descriptions of the World*. Europe was amazed at what Marco Polo had found and seen in China. At that time, China's achievements were more advanced than those of Europe's.

In the second phase, Europe overtook China and the rest of East Asia. Powered by the Enlightenment and the Industrial Revolution, Europe soared while an ossified East declined. Much of East Asia was either colonised or dominated by Europe in some form or other.

In the third encounter, Europe and East Asia are dealing with each other as approximate equals. In 1965, Europe and Asia accounted for 25 per cent and 9 per cent of world GDP respectively. In purchasing power parity (PPP) terms, the figures in 1994 showed that the combined GDP of the European Union's 15 member countries was US$6,728 billion and US$7,656 billion for Asia and the Oceania. At an annual average growth rate of 5–6 per cent, East Asia's GDP would be 40 per cent of world output in 2020. In the area of trade, Asia accounted for 10 per cent of world trade while Europe accounted for 44 per cent in 1970. In 1994, Asia's share increased to 19 per cent, while Europe's share declined to 38 per cent.

Rationale for the Summit

Why did Singapore Prime Minister Goh Chok Tong propose the holding of an Asia–Europe Summit? He did it for the following reasons.

First, the world economy is now being driven by three locomotives: North America, Western Europe and East Asia. Between North America and Western Europe, there exists a thick web of human and institutional links, from the North Atlantic Treaty Organisation (NATO), Organisation for Security and Cooperation in Europe (OSCE) to the Spoleto Festival of Two Worlds. There are also growing links between North America and East Asia. In recent years, besides the various bilateral security ties between the US and some of the East Asian countries, leaders of East Asia and North America have begun building multilateral linkages across the Pacific. The Asia–Pacific Economic Cooperation (APEC) forum is one such example. There is, however, no equivalent multilateral institutional linkage between the European Union (EU) and East Asia. The Asia–Europe Summit in Bangkok is the first step towards filling this void.

Second, unlike North America and Europe, East Asia and Europe are under-trading and under-investing in each other's economies. The European Union's investments in East Asia are smaller than those of the US and those of intra-regional Asian investors. The reverse is also true. Apart from Japan, East Asia's investment in the EU is negligible. In 1994, the 10 countries[a] in East Asia accounted for 25 per cent of North America's total trade but only 8 per cent of EU's trade. The conclusion is obvious. Our private sectors are under-trading with and under-investing in each other. Our governments can facilitate this process. They can give political support for a broader and deeper engagement between the two regions.

Third, Europe and Asia need each other. Rapid growth in East Asia is creating huge demands for capital investment,

---

[a] These 10 East Asian countries are Brunei, Indonesia, Malaysia, the Philippines, Singapore, Thailand, Vietnam, China, Japan and South Korea.

technology, management know-how, and consumer goods and services. The World Bank has estimated that in infrastructure alone, developing East Asia needs investments of between US$1.3 trillion and US$1.5 trillion for the period 1995 to 2004. Europe needs Asia's markets. East Asia is already an important market for European companies such as Airbus and Daimler Benz. More can be done. With competition becoming increasingly global, European companies need to establish their presence in East Asia. They need to enter into strategic alliances with Asian companies in order to remain competitive and succeed in a world economy which is increasingly globalised.

Fourth, the EU and East Asia need to reassure each other of their mutual commitment to uphold the regime of free trade under the aegis of the World Trade Organisation (WTO) and to the practice of open regionalism. Asians want to be assured that a united Europe will not become a Fortress Europe. The EU wants to be assured by East Asia that APEC will remain committed to the concept of open regionalism.

Fifth, there is a need for increased intellectual exchange and dialogue between Europeans and Asians on a whole spectrum of transnational issues, such as good governance, democracy, human rights, reform of the United Nations (UN), nuclear proliferation, international crime and the environment. We want to avoid Samuel Huntington's prognosis of a civilisational clash between Europe and Asia. Therefore, we need to create more opportunities for European and Asian non-governmental organisations (NGOs) and individuals such as intellectuals, journalists, young leaders and artistes to meet. Such meetings must be held on the basis of mutual respect and mutual learning.

What Did the Bangkok Summit Achieve?

The inaugural Asia–Europe Summit in Bangkok achieved the following:

- It provided the 16 leaders of Europe and the 10 leaders of East Asia the opportunity to meet and to establish rapport;

- It provided opportunities for bilateral meetings, for example, between President Suharto of Indonesia and the Prime Minister of Portugal;
- It generated greater awareness and understanding on the part of Europeans regarding Asia, its economic dynamism, and its ability to get things done;
- It adopted a series of concrete proposals and decisions. These include the drawing up of an Investment Promotion Action Plan and a Trade Facilitation Action Plan, the decision to establish an Asia–Europe Environmental Technology Centre to facilitate technical cooperation in the area of the environment, and an Asia–Europe Foundation to facilitate intellectual, cultural and people-to-people exchanges; and
- It has institutionalised the process with the commitment to hold the next Summit in London in 1998, and the subsequent one in Seoul in 2000. Other Ministerial and Senior Officials Meetings were also agreed upon.

Conclusion

With all the above commitments, I can only conclude that a rich and fruitful relationship lies ahead for Asia and Europe. With better mutual understanding and learning, the scope for cooperation is tremendous.

(*Speech delivered at the Royal Institute of International Affairs in London, UK on 22 April 1996.*)

East Asia, Western Europe and North America
A New Trinity in International Relations

Introduction

Until a few years ago, Japan was the only successful country in Asia. After the Second World War, Japan emerged from the ashes of war like the legendary bird, the phoenix. By the 1980s, Japan had become a powerhouse of the world economy and a leading nation of the world. This was the logic which led to the inclusion of Japan in the Group of Seven. It also led to the establishment of the Trilateral Commission, a non-governmental organisation which brings together some of the best minds of the United States, Western Europe and Japan.

Japan is no longer the only successful country in Asia. Its success has been emulated by other countries in East Asia. The first group to take off after Japan consisted of the four newly industrialising economies (NIEs), Hong Kong, South Korea, Singapore and Taiwan. The second group to take off comprised Malaysia, Thailand, Indonesia and the Philippines, often referred to as the ASEAN 4, and China. Finally, at the back of the flock of flying geese, we have the latecomers, Vietnam, Myanmar, Laos and Cambodia.

The rise of East Asia has been so rapid and dramatic that it has escaped the attention of many friends in the West. It is startling even to an Asian like me. Three decades ago, in 1965, East Asia accounted for only 9 per cent of the world economy.

In 1995, East Asia accounted for 25 per cent of the world's gross national product (GNP), on nominal terms, whereas the European Union and North America each accounted for 29 per cent.

The Thesis

It is against this background that I have chosen to speak on the topic: "East Asia, Western Europe and North America: A New Trinity in International Relations". I will assert the following five propositions. First, economically, we live in a trilateral world. Second, it is in the interest of world peace and security that we establish cordial and cooperative relations between the three power centres, namely, North America, Western Europe and East Asia. Third, there are strong ties between Western Europe and North America. There are growing ties between North America and East Asia. The weak link is the relationship between Western Europe and East Asia. To have a strong and equal partnership in the trilateral world, there is a need therefore to strengthen this weak link in all fields. Fourth, East Asia and Western Europe have many points of convergence. There are many opportunities for the two regions to cooperate for their mutual benefit. Fifth, Western Europe and East Asia should also cooperate to maintain international peace, to uphold free trade, to expand economic opportunities and to protect the global commons and the environment.

A Trilateral World

The world economy is being driven by three equally powerful engines, Western Europe, North America and East Asia. Since the world economy has three co-drivers it is important for the three regional economies to remain open and outward-oriented. We must prevent any trade war among them or between any two of them. A few years ago, just before the EU implemented the single European market, there were fears in Asia and America that Europe might turn inward and become Fortress Europe.

Such fears have proved to be unfounded. Similarly, many Europeans had expressed the fear that APEC countries, which account for 40 per cent of world trade, might turn inward and shut Europe out of the Asia–Pacific. This has not happened. On the contrary, APEC is the first and only regional trading arrangement which is committed to the concept of open regionalism.

East Asia, Western Europe and North America should uphold the principle and practice of free trade and work together to strengthen the World Trade Organisation (WTO). This means, among other things, that our respective regional trading arrangements should conform to the principles of WTO, that we should abstain from the temptation of unilateralism, and that we should comply with the results of the WTO dispute settlement procedures. It also means that we should accept the principle of comparative economic advantage which is the economic underpinning of business relations. We should welcome foreign investment and resist the evil of economic nationalism.

As a further development, ASEAN is exploring the feasibility of linking the ASEAN Free Trade Area (AFTA) and the Australia–New Zealand Common Economic Relations Trade Agreement. There are also indications of interest in exploring the possibility of linking the North American Free Trade Area (NAFTA) and AFTA. Such inter-regional economic linkages should be welcomed so long as they do not discriminate against others.

The Three Sides of the Triangle

The three regional economies are linked to one another by a triangle. The strongest side of the triangle is that between Western Europe and North America. Ties of history, kinship and culture have created a thick web of human and institutional relationships and networks between Europe and America. There is a high degree of familiarity and comfort between Europeans and Americans.

The second strongest side of the triangle is that between North America and East Asia. In the past 50 years, the United

States has fought three wars in East Asia. In the past 10 years, its trade with East Asia has exceeded its trade with Western Europe. Five times as many students from East Asia study in America than in Europe. The Asian–American community is the fastest growing community in the US population. As a result of APEC and other common institutions such as the ASEAN Regional Forum (ARF) there is a growing sense of a Pacific Economic Community.

Although the relationship between Europe and Asia goes back 700 years, it is the weakest side of the triangle. The number of Asian students going to study in Europe has been declining compared with the stream flowing to the United States. The flow of students from Western Europe to East Asia is a mere trickle. After the withdrawal of France from Indochina and the United Kingdom from east of Suez, Western Europe lost interest in Asia. Compared with the US, Western Europe is under-trading with and under-investing in East Asia.

In 1995, US trade with East Asia was 30 per cent of its total trade with the world. In contrast, EU's trade with East Asia was only 8 per cent of its total trade with the world. As far as investment is concerned, Japan, the US and the EU have provided about half the foreign direct investment (FDI) to developing East Asia. Of the three providers, the EU is the smallest. In 1993, the EU accounted for 13 per cent of total FDI stock in developing East Asia whereas Japan accounted for 21 per cent and the US 14 per cent.

Europe and Asia: A Journey of Rediscovery

The Bangkok Summit of 1 March 1996 marked the beginning of a journey of rediscovery between Europe and East Asia. At the Asia–Europe Meeting (ASEM) in Bangkok, the 26 leaders decided to begin a new and comprehensive engagement between Asia and Europe. They decided to build a Euro–Asian house. This house will have four pillars. The first pillar consists of the growing rapport and relationship between our political leaders.

The second pillar consists of the networking taking place between our officials. The third pillar consists of the links between our two business communities. The fourth pillar consists of the engagement between our two civil societies. The Asia–Europe Foundation has been tasked to build the fourth pillar.

The Role of Business in Linking Asia and Europe

Business has played and is playing a central role in integrating the world. The role of the ASEM governments is to reduce barriers and to create a conducive business environment which would enable the business enterprises of Asia and Europe to forge links with one another. The potential for each side to do more with the other is tremendous. East Asia is the world's fastest growing region. Europe, on the other hand, represents the world's largest, most integrated and sophisticated economy. European companies should capitalise on its increasing sophistication to tap into the fast-growing markets of East Asia. Only then can they enhance their profitability and expand their global market shares.

Why are European companies not more active in Asia? There are several reasons. There is a knowledge gap. Many European companies lack in-depth knowledge about the Asian markets. In Asia, it is as important to "know who" as to "know how". European companies therefore need help in order to meet suitable joint-venture partners who could show them the way in Asia. This is particularly important for small and medium enterprises. It is also important for European companies to understand the culture of doing business in various Asian countries.

Another reason could be that in some Asian countries, there is a lack of transparency and of a clear and stable regulatory framework. Asian governments need to take urgent action to improve their business environment.

The process of building Euro–Asian business networks have been given a strong boost by the first Asia–Europe Business Forum (AEBF), hosted by France in October 1996. The AEBF was a success and a decision has been made to make it a regular event. The next AEBF will be hosted by Thailand in November 1997. Other initiatives to build business relationship have also surfaced. The first Asia–Europe Business Conference was successfully held in Jakarta in July 1997. In November 1997, Singapore will host the ASEAN–EU Partenariat. This will bring together about 250 European and 500 ASEAN small and medium enterprises. In March 1998, Italy intends to host the first Asia–Europe Conference of Small and Medium Enterprises in Naples.

To Avert a Clash of Civilisations

The Asia–Europe Foundation (ASEF) has been charged with the mandate of promoting better mutual understanding between Asia and Europe through greater intellectual, cultural and people-to-people exchanges. In his provocative new book, *The Clash of Civilizations and the Remaking of the World Order*, Samuel Huntington writes: "The future of both peace and civilisation depends upon understanding and cooperation among the political, spiritual, and intellectual leaders of the world's major civilisations". Asia and Europe are the homes of several ancient and rich civilisations. There is tremendous scope for bringing together the leading intellectual, artistic, spiritual and young leaders of our two regions to dialogue, to write, to exhibit and to perform together. We could produce new blossoms from the cross fertilisation between our rich civilisations. Not only would a clash of civilisations be averted, but an enriched and peaceful new world would await us.

(*Speech to the Annual Meeting of Finnish Ambassadors in Helsinki, Finland on 2 September 1997.*)

Asia's Future and
Its Relations with the West

Asia Defined

I have been invited to speak on the topic: "Asia's Future and Its Relations with the Western World". Asia is a huge continent. It is a continent of great diversity. Unlike Latin America, it has no common language, religion or culture. For the purpose of this lecture I shall use the word "Asia" to mean Pacific Asia or East Asia. East Asia is made up of two sub-regions, Northeast Asia and Southeast Asia. Northeast Asia comprises China, Japan, Korea, Taiwan and Hong Kong. The five economies are all members of Asia–Pacific Economic Cooperation (APEC). Southeast Asia consists of ten countries, nine of which are members of the Association of Southeast Asian Nations (ASEAN). The nine members of ASEAN are Brunei, Indonesia, Laos, Malaysia, Myanmar (Burma), the Philippines, Singapore, Thailand and Vietnam. Cambodia is not yet a member of ASEAN. Seven of the ten countries of Southeast Asia are members of APEC.

An Asian Miracle?

Before I discuss Asia's future, I would like to say a few words about Asia's past and present. For Asians of my generation, the Asian miracle is a reality not a myth. As a young man I had studied at Cambridge University and Harvard University in the 1960s. If a British friend had asked me at Cambridge whether I could imagine a day in my lifetime when Singapore's per capita income would overtake that of Britain I would have said, "Impossible". If an American friend had asked me at Harvard whether I could imagine a day in my lifetime when Singapore's infant mortality rate and maternal mortality rate would be lower than those of the United States I would have replied, "Not in my lifetime". Miraculously, what I had thought impossible to achieve in one generation have come to pass. It is not just Singapore which has experienced this miracle. Most of the countries of East Asia have experienced a similar transformation.

Let me share with you a few facts which I have extracted from UNDP's 1997 Human Development Index. East Asia has a remarkable record in poverty reduction. The World Bank has estimated that the region succeeded in reducing the number of its poor from 716.8 million in 1975 to 345.7 million in 1995, a rate which is unprecedented in history. Adult illiteracy has been substantially reduced or eliminated. Public health has improved, as reflected in life expectancy, infant mortality and maternal mortality rates. Singapore's infant mortality rate declined from 36 per thousand in 1960 to 5 per thousand in 1994. East Asia's success in economic development has been translated into social progress for the great majority of the people. The East Asian model of development can be described as growth with equity.

East Asia's rise in the world economy has been dramatic. In 1965, East Asia's share of the world economy was 9 per cent. In 1995, its share rose to 25 per cent. In that same year, North America and the European Union each accounted for 29 per cent. Assuming that East Asia grew at an annual average rate of 5 per cent and North America and the European Union at an annual average rate of 2.5 per cent, East Asia would catch up with the other two regions in the year 2000. By the year 2025, East Asia's economy would be larger than those of North America and the European Union combined.

Or an Asian Mirage?

I have painted a very rosy picture of East Asia's achievements in the last 30 years. How do I explain the recent turmoil in Southeast Asia which brought down the values of the Thai baht, the Malaysian ringgit, the Indonesian rupiah, the Filipino peso and all of our stock exchanges? The crisis began in Thailand. Thailand's economy had been growing confidently for a decade at 6 to 8 per cent. The economic fundamentals looked good. Why was there a loss of confidence in the Thai baht and in the Thai stock exchange? The reason was that because of poor regulation, the Thai financial sector had become unsound. Thai financial institutions had borrowed too much "hot" money and had made too many loans to real estate speculators. The situation resembled the bubble economy of Japan in the 1980s. The Thai bubble burst and there was a crisis of confidence in the Thai baht and the Thai stock exchange. After a futile attempt to fight the market, the Thai Central Bank decided to float the baht.

When the Mexican peso collapsed a few years ago, it was like a virus which infected all the neighbours' currencies. I believe you called it the "tequila" effect. In a similar way, the collapse of the Thai baht had a regional effect which we call the "*tomyam*" effect, named after the famous Thai soup, "*tomyam*". As a result, all the regional currencies lost value, although to varying degrees, and all our stock exchanges were devastated. In contrast, Northeast Asia was unaffected except for the Korean won.

Lessons Learnt

What lessons have I learnt from the recent crisis? First, I have learnt that the idea that we have one integrated financial market is a reality. No country or region can insulate itself from the world financial market. This means that we are exposed every day to the market's judgement of our economic performance. Second, in this new world, the market is more powerful than the government. Gone are the days when a powerful government or a group of powerful governments could determine a currency's exchange rate. Now, the money in the hands of the foreign exchange dealers is more than in the coffers of the central banks. No central bank or group of central banks can defeat the market. Third, high growth is no substitute for maintaining sound macroecnomic and fiscal policies. If you lose sight of this imperative the market will punish you.

Is the Miracle Over?

Is the miracle over? The Asian Development Bank (ADB), the World Bank, and the International Monetary Fund (IMF) do not think so. Thailand will face the greatest challenge of putting its house in order but its economy is still expected to grow this year at 2.5 to 3 per cent. Malaysia has revised its growth forecast for this year from 8 to 7 per cent. Singapore expects that it will still be able to achieve its 7 per cent growth target. Most analysts believe that the region will continue to grow at between 5 and 7 per cent per annum.

However, the challenge for most of Southeast Asia is to move from low-tech, labour-intensive and low-value-added industries to high-tech, high-value-added industries. This requires massive investment in the education and training of our work force. Unless we can upgrade the skills of our work force, solve our infrastructural bottlenecks and pursue sound macroeconomic and fiscal policies, the East Asian miracle will be in jeopardy.

Asia's Future: Two Scenarios

The Optimistic Scenario

What is the future of Asia? Nothing in life is certain. The future is inherently unpredictable. It is tempting but unsafe to make linear projections. Therefore, although mainstream economists predict that East Asia can continue to grow at an annual average rate of 5 per cent for the next 20 years, it is better to describe this as the optimistic scenario. If the optimistic scenario comes true, East Asia will be transformed into a region of prosperity. This will, in turn, lead to a cultural renaissance. Civil society will be strengthened. Political institutions will become more open, participatory and accountable. The rule of law will prevail over the rule of man. Eventually, there could be an East Asian model, combining the best from the West and the best of the East Asian heritage.

The Pessimistic Scenario

The East Asian success story could have a sad ending for several reasons:

First, if we become intoxicated with our own success and start to mismanage our economies, pursuing unsound macro-economic or fiscal policies and eroding our strong economic fundamentals such as high savings, high investment and good work ethic. Or if we refuse to make adjustments and resolve our infrastructural problems and upgrade the skills of our work force to stay competitive.

Second, if the international trading system breaks down. Although unlikely, it is possible to envisage a scenario in which the WTO collapses and NAFTA, the EU and East Asia emerge as inward-looking rival trading blocs. In such a scenario, trade wars will occur, world trade will shrink and the East Asian economies will be badly affected.

Third, if the region becomes unstable. There is a close nexus between economics and security. The East Asian economic miracle has been made possible by the relative peace which the region has enjoyed over the past three decades. The peace and stability of the region have been underpinned by the commitment of the United States and by its military presence in the region. This happy state of affairs could change for the worse. For example, the United States may decide to withdraw from the region. This will leave a vacuum which China and Japan may try to fill. This will start an arms race between those two powers. Another possibility is that relations between China and the United States could deteriorate. It is possible to envisage a new Cold War between the US and Japan, on one side, and China, on the other. If the region becomes unstable, this will have a direct impact on its investment climate and on its economic prospects.

Asia's Relations with the West

How will Asia relate to the West? If Asia is to continue its path of development and become rich and powerful, will it turn its back on the West? Is there any merit in the Huntington thesis on the clash of civilisations? Or will Asia work together with the West to build a stable and peaceful new world order?

"Yankee, please don't go home"

There is rising nationalism in some East Asian countries, particularly China. Throughout East Asia, there is a new-found sense of self-respect and pride in their cultural heritage. This is understandable because for several centuries, when Asia was poor and backward, Asians had a sense of inferiority towards the West. Young Asians no longer feel inferior to the West. They did not live under colonial rule. Many of them studied at the best universities in the West and proved that they were as good as their Western classmates. There is therefore a rising sense of pride. Fortunately, this sense of pride is generally not accompanied by anti-West sentiments or xenophobia. For example, no one in Southeast Asia is campaigning to expel the Americans. On the contrary, the Southeast Asians are saying to Washington, "Yankee, please don't go home".

Building Bridges — APEC and ASEM

What is the strategic vision of Asian thinkers towards the West? The majority in Asia believe that we live in a trilateral world. The world economy is being co-driven by three powerful regional economies, namely, North America, Western Europe and East

Asia. East Asians want to build bridges connecting East Asia with North America and East Asia with Western Europe. This is why we are committed to APEC's success. We see APEC as serving both important economic and political objectives. Economically, APEC links the two most dynamic regions of the world. Politically, it serves to prevent the Pacific Ocean from being divided between an Asian rim and an American rim. We wish to prevent a repeat of the Pacific War.

For the same reason, East Asia convened the first Asia–Europe Summit in Bangkok in March 1996. The summit was attended by the 15 leaders of the European Union and the President of the European Commission, together with 10 Asian leaders. The summit has opened a new chapter in the 700 year-old relationship between Asia and Europe. There is tremendous potential in this relationship as Asia and Europe look at each other with new eyes and see each other as partners and friends rather than adversaries.

Conclusion

Let me bring my lecture to a close. I will sum up by recapitulating the following 5 points. First, I have used the term "Asia" to refer only to East Asia. Second, in the past 30 years, many of the countries and peoples of East Asia have lived through a miraculous transformation which catapulted them from the minor league of nations to the major league. Third, the recent setbacks in the currency and stock markets of Southeast Asia are unlikely to derail the train from the fast track. Fourth, if the optimistic scenario comes true, East Asia's economy will be as big as those of NAFTA and the EU by the year 2000 and will be bigger than North America and Western Europe combined in 2025. Fifth, Asians do not wish to form an exclusive club and turn their back on the West. On the contrary, East Asia wishes to broaden and deepen its relationship with North America and Western Europe. We wish to be a good partner of the West. However, we wish to be treated with respect. There are and will always be cultural differences between East Asia and the West but we share more commonalities than we have differences. Besides, we live in an increasingly interdependent and integrated world, driven by the forces of globalisation, multinational business, technology, human mobility and the global environment. I therefore do not believe that we are headed towards a war of civilisation between the West and the East. On the contrary, I think the world is headed towards a more cosmopolitan millennium in which national boundaries will mean less and less and in which multiculturalism will be our common creed.

(*Lecture given at the Eduardo Frei Foundation, Santiago, Chile on 1 October 1997.*)

BUILDING BRIDGES
Business Ties, Cultural Exchange and Intellectual Dialogue

Commerce, culture and communication determine the contours of Asian–European relations. The three forces do not always coincide, but the two continents have enough in common on which to build a balanced relationship, and a new world. ASEM (Asia–Europe Meeting), ASEAN (Association of Southeast Asian Nations) and the EU (European Union) are more than familiar acronyms: They embody the institutional bases of the intercontinental engagement. The following essays flesh out the points of contact and compromise between the two regions, and show how they can limit the lines of divergence.

Building Bridges among the Young
The Message from Miyazaki

The Miyazaki Symposium has been co-sponsored by the Ministry of Foreign Affairs (Gaimusho) of Japan and the Asia–Europe Foundation (ASEF). The Gaimusho is the senior partner and ASEF is the junior partner. Deputy Minister Yanai has requested me to attempt an overview of the Symposium in about twenty minutes. Although I have listened to the discussions in all seven workshops, and I have read the reports of the seven chairpersons, I will probably fail to do justice to the Symposium. I must therefore ask for your forgiveness in advance.

Let me begin by thanking the Governor and the citizens of Miyazaki for inviting the Symposium to meet here. The environment is both beautiful and congenial. We have been happy here, except for golfers among us. The golfers think that the organisers are sadistic people. Why else should they hold the symposium at a resort with such a beautiful golf course and not include time in our programme for a daily game of golf? After all, the golfers from Southeast Asia know that the best discussions at a meeting often take place on a golf course.

We must thank the Government of Japan and Prime Minister Hashimoto in particular, for having taken the initiative to convene the first symposium of young leaders from Asia and Europe. As Prime Minister Carlsson pointed out in his keynote address, this Symposium is important for three reasons. If one of our tasks is to build bridges from the 20th century to the 21st century, it is right to involve young bridge-builders in the process, for it is they who will be leaders of the 21st century. Young leaders are likely to be more open-minded, more creative and more receptive to new ideas than older leaders. This Symposium is not a one-off affair. We have begun a process which will be continued next year in Austria and in other ASEM countries in the years to come.

For the past two days, 110 young leaders from Asia and Europe have met in Miyazaki. They come from 25 countries, in two continents, with a variety of backgrounds. Yet, almost instantly, they have developed rapport with one another and the group has developed a club-like atmosphere. In the workshops and the brainstorming sessions, I observed that the young leaders engaged in frank and serious discussions but in a collegial atmosphere with the spirit of mutual respect and mutual learning. This is what the organisers had hoped for. If nothing else was achieved I would have said that the Miyazaki Symposium was a success because the process was a success. To modify a quote from Marshall McLuhan, "The process is the message." However, the young leaders have exceeded my expectations. They have arrived at many points of convergence and a set of conclusions and recommendations. I will attempt to distill them into what I call "The Message from Miyazaki". What is the message from Miyazaki?

First, the young leaders agreed with the observation by Dr Han Sung-joo in his keynote address that: "The first summit meeting between Asia and Europe, which took place in Bangkok just one year ago, was Europe's way of rediscovering Asia and acknowledging it as a partner in prosperity and peace. For Asia, ASEM represented its acceptance of these European gestures and recognition of Europe as a key pillar of Asian development and security".

Second, the young leaders also agreed with Dr Han's point that ASEM is not and should not be viewed as being at the expense of Europe's transatlantic ties or East Asia's transpacific ties. On the contrary, ASEM is the third side of a triangle linking the three centres of the world economy, namely, North America, Western Europe and East Asia. The spirit of ASEM is trilateralism.

Third, Asia and Europe are two regions with very rich cultures and civilisations. What is culture? Culture is a living force. It gives a human being his identity. It provides him with a frame of reference to relate to his family, his society, his natural environment and his God. Culture provides us with a moral compass to navigate the journey of life and the resilience to stand up to adversity. It would be desirable for the young peoples of Asia and Europe to learn each other's languages and cultures, to have the experience of studying and working in each other's regions and of staying in each other's homes. Many modalities to do so were discussed. It was also agreed that we should use the fine arts, music, dance, theatre, film, literature, painting, sculpture, photography and all other art forms to inspire and unite our peoples.

Fourth, we agree that economic development and the accumulation of wealth is not an end in itself. It is a means to improve the welfare of our peoples. It is to give our peoples a better life. In Europe, this means, among other things, reducing unemployment. In Asia, it means eradication of poverty and the increase in social and gender equity. In both regions, welfare also means the right to live in a clean and healthy environment. Economies in Asia and Europe both face the challenge of upgrading in order to remain competitive. They must also manage the impact of globalisation, which produces both winners and losers. What is the solution? One answer lies in the need to invest in education and training.

Fifth, we reaffirm our faith and commitment to the ideal and practice of free trade. We agreed to support the WTO, to implement the results of the Singapore Ministerial Conference, and to strengthen its efficacy. We look forward to the early accession of China to the WTO. We agreed that regional integration and liberalisation in Europe and Asia should be compatible with the WTO, and should result in the progressive lowering of external barriers. We agree with Dr Carlsson when he said that turning inwards is not an option.

Sixth, we are impressed by the burst of energy and enthusiasm which the Bangkok Summit has unleashed. Apart from the Summit, the ministers of foreign affairs, finance and trade have met or will be meeting. The private sector, represented by the Business Forum and the Business Conference, has become an intrinsic part of the ASEM process. About forty other projects have been implemented. The process is evolving and organic. It is hoped that the Vision Group, which will be appointed by ASEM II in London next year, will come up with a cooperation framework which will give the process a needed sense of coherence and structure. In the absence of an ASEM secretariat, ASEF should consider playing the role of ASEM's clearing house.

Seventh, the role of the private sector, the partnership between the private sector and the government, and the social responsibility of business were the subjects of a very rich discussion. It was agreed that international business should cooperate with the host government in training and upgrading the skills of the local work force. It was also agreed that business should work with the government to achieve sustainable development. Governments in both regions should create a business environment which is conducive to foreign investments. Asian governments should do more to develop their capital markets.

Eighth, it was agreed that, as we live in an interdependent world, it is not possible to separate the security of Europe from the security of Asia. Upheavals in one region, for example, Bosnia or Indochina, will have an impact on the other. Our organising concept must be the concept of common security. Asians welcome the role which Europe is playing in the ASEAN Regional Forum (ARF). The ARF and other such multilateral fora are not intended to supplant but to complement existing bilateral defence arrangements and the central role which the US plays in both Asia and Europe. Europeans welcome the role which some Asians, such as Yasushi Akashi in the former Yugoslavia, Han Sung-joo in Cyprus, and myself in the Baltics, have played in trying to resolve disputes and conflicts in Europe. We agreed to cooperate to strengthen international institutions, such as the United Nations, and to combat threats to our common security posed by terrorism, weapons proliferation, international crime, the drug menace, and the AIDS epidemic.

Ninth, Asia and Europe must cooperate to harness the wonders of multimedia. We can use cyberspace to build bridges of information, knowledge and understanding between net-citizens. We must, individually and collectively, create contents, websites, films and television programmes. We should aspire to be not just consumers but content providers. ASEM and ASEF should use information technology as tools in their work.

Tenth, we agreed with Dr Carlsson that Asia and Europe cannot ignore the rest of the world. Shrunk by globalisation, information technology, and jet travel, the world has become our neighbourhood. Asia and Europe must therefore cooperate to maintain peace and order, to expand economic opportunities for peoples everywhere, especially in the least developed countries, to protect the global commons, and to protect the environment. In short, to build a better world.

(Speech delivered at the Closing Plenary of the Asia–Europe Young Leaders Symposium in Miyazaki, Japan, on 12 March 1997.)

Towards a Productive Asia–Europe Business Relations

Dear Chairman, Ladies and Gentlemen,

I am very pleased to be with you this morning. I feel honoured to have been paired with Sir Charles Powell. Sir Charles was, for many years, a close lieutenant of the Iron Lady, Margaret Thatcher. Recently, my Prime Minister and the British Prime Minister met at the United Nations in New York. Turning to the young man seated on his left, Prime Minister Blair introduced him to my Prime Minister as Sir Charles Powell's younger brother, Jonathan. With a smile on his face, Tony Blair said, "Every British Prime Minister needs a Powell!"

A Hopeful New World

I would like to begin with an overview of the world in which we live. It is very different from the world a decade ago. What are some of the salient characteristics of the new world?

Economic Trilateralism

First, economically, we live in a trilateral world. For the first time in history, the world economy is being driven by three approximately equal regional economies, namely, North America, Western Europe and East Asia. Each region contributes approximately 25 per cent to the world's GNP. World peace and prosperity therefore require that we build a strong triangle connecting the three economic power centres. Asia, Europe and America must avoid the temptation to play one against the other. We must be united by a spirit of trilateralism.

Towards a Borderless World

Second, we live in a world in which the barriers to the flow of goods, services, capital, technology, information and human talent are progressively falling. We do not yet live in a borderless world but we are heading in that general direction. Asia, Europe and America should unite to maintain this trend and to fight against the ideas of those who would like to take us back to the discredited ideology of economic nationalism. We should support the World Trade Organisation (WTO). We should ensure that our respective regional trading arrangements, such as the European Union, the ASEAN Free Trade Area and APEC, are consistent with our primary allegiance to the WTO.

Business as Integrator

Third, business has played and is playing a central role in integrating the world. Let us take APEC as an example. APEC is emerging as an economic community because of the strong economic linkages which exist between and among the 18 APEC economies. These economic linkages are forged, not by the government or the bureaucracy, but by the daily decisions of a multitude of business enterprises. In the same way, the role of the governments of Asia and Europe is to reduce barriers and to create a conducive business environment which would enable the business enterprises of Asia and Europe to forge links with one another. In our new world, business is often marching ahead of government in seizing opportunities, building comparative advantage and synergy, and creating links between enterprises, economies, countries and regions.

The Weak Side of the Triangle

Let me return to my triangle. When we examine the three sides of the triangle, we are struck by the fact that the weakest side of the triangle is that between East Asia and Western Europe. Transatlantic and transpacific ties, including those of trade and investment, are stronger than those between East Asia and Western Europe. The conclusion is obvious: Asia and Europe are under-trading with, and under-investing in, each other's economies. Why is this the case despite the fact that East Asia is the world's fastest growing region, and the European Union is the world's most integrated and sophisticated economy? Why are European companies not more active in Asia? Why are Asian companies not more active in Europe? There are several reasons.

Knowledge Gap

First, there is a knowledge gap. Many European companies lack in-depth knowledge about the Asian markets. In Asia, it is as important to "know who" as to "know how". European companies therefore need help in order to meet suitable joint-venture partners who could show them the way in Asia. This is particularly important for the small and medium enterprises. It is also important for European companies to understand the cultures of doing business in the various Asian countries.

Fear of Europe

Second, Asian investors are sometimes hesitant to invest in Europe. Apart from the UK, Ireland and, to a certain extent, the Netherlands, the European business environment is perceived by Asians as containing some negative elements, for example, labour inflexibility and high unit production costs. Asian companies also suffer from a knowledge gap. They lack detailed knowledge of developments and opportunities in Europe.

An Asian Problem

Third, one factor which in some parts of Asia discourages European investment is the lack of transparency and of a clear and stable regulatory framework. Asian governments should take urgent action to create a more conducive business environment to attract European investment.

Realising the Business Potential

What then can we do to increase the two-way flow of business between East Asia and Western Europe? I have three suggestions.

Networking

First, we should continue the process we have begun of building Euro–Asian business networks, both at the inter-regional level and bilaterally among all the different ASEM countries. The first Asia–Europe Business Forum, hosted by France in October 1996, was a success. More business initiatives and networking opportunities should be encouraged.

Role of ASEM Governments

Second, the ASEM governments should, individually and collectively, work to create a more conducive business environment in their respective regions. We must uphold the ideal and practice of free trade. We must emphasise that the economic underpinning of business relations is comparative economic advantage. We must work to level the playing field for greater transparency and predictability, remove excessive regulation, and develop a culture of welcoming foreign direct investment.

ASEF's Contributions

Third, the term "business" in the Chinese language consists of two characters, "sheng yi" meaning life and benefit. Business relations are therefore closely related to life and to its benefits.

There is therefore a close nexus between business and culture. Better cultural understanding between East Asia and Western Europe will support successful business relations between our two regions. This is where the Asia–Europe Foundation can make a contribution. We intend to convene a meeting of leading news editors this October in Luxembourg. We need to persuade the mass media in our two regions to report each other in a more accurate and balanced manner and to discard old stereotypes. We also intend to bring together the deans of the leading business schools of Asia and Europe. We hope that this could lead to a greater flow of MBA students from Europe to Asia and *vice versa*. In February 1998, we will be co-sponsoring a forum which will examine, *inter alia*, the business cultures of East Asia and Western Europe. The mission of the Asia–Europe Foundation is an ambitious one. It is to create better mutual understanding between Europe and Asia by building bridges between our two civil societies. We hope that the business community will support us in this noble mission.

(*Paper delivered at the Asia–Europe Business Conference held in Jakarta on 9 July 1997.*)

Towards a Common Economic Agenda in the Post-Crisis Era

Introduction

East Asia is suffering from the worst economic crisis of the past 30 years. In the midst of such adversity, is it presumptuous of me to talk about East Asia and West Europe having a common economic agenda? Does Western Europe still view East Asia as a valuable economic power? Will East Asia recover and remain as an attractive economic partner?

Will East Asia Bounce Back?

Will East Asia bounce back? A majority of the pundits seem to agree that East Asia will recover, if not in 1999 then in 2000. However, different countries are likely to bounce back at different speeds. There is already light at the end of the tunnel for Thailand and South Korea.

In Thailand and South Korea, the baht and the won have stabilised. Interest rates have declined. Both countries are enjoying trade and current account surpluses. The fact that investor confidence has returned can be shown by the fact that foreign direct investments (FDI) have increased in 1998. In the case of Thailand, FDI for the first six months of 1998 was US$3 billion, representing an increase of 100 per cent over the corresponding period in 1997. In the case of South Korea, FDI for the first eight months of 1998 was US$2.7 billion, representing an increase of 36 per cent over the corresponding period in 1997.

The bottom line is that East Asia is on the mend. European investors who have a medium-term to long-term perspective will find many interesting opportunities in East Asia.

New Investment Opportunities for Europe

Because of the crisis and the IMF conditionalities, economies such as Thailand, Korea and the Philippines are more open today than they have ever been. Their banks and businesses need capital. Many of their companies are looking for investors, partners and allies. There are therefore many opportunities for European investors in banking, other service industries, manufacturing and resource-based industries. At the second ASEM Summit held in London in April 1998, European leaders pledged to send investment missions to visit East Asia. Some such missions have already visited the region. I urge Europe to send more investment missions to East Asia.

Keep Europe's Markets Open

In the short term, East Asia will export more to Europe than it will import from Europe. Europe will therefore suffer a trade deficit with East Asia. This may provoke protectionist elements in Europe to agitate against rising imports from East Asia. I hope that European leaders will have the courage to resist such protectionist pressures. They could explain to their citizens that until the crisis hit East Asia, the region imported more from the European Union than the United States. When East Asia recovers it will again be Europe's largest export market. Politically, it is important for Europe to share the burden with the United States in absorbing exports from East Asia. It is a pity that Japan, the second largest economy in the world, is itself in a state of crisis.

The Advent of the Euro

The euro was successfully launched on 1 January 1999. This has created two important opportunities for East Asia. First, the euro will become an important international currency, along with the US dollar and the Japanese yen. Many East Asian countries will be able to diversify their foreign exchange reserves by including the euro. In managing their currencies against a trade-weighted basket of currencies, they will be able to include the euro as one such currency. The second opportunity is that the euro zone has created a larger bond market than the United States. Asian governments and companies, with good credit rating, will be able to raise capital in Europe.

A Common Trade Agenda

East Asia and Western Europe should cooperate at the WTO to maintain its primacy, to maintain the momentum towards trade and investment liberalisation, and to facilitate the greater flows of trade and investment between the two regions. An immediate goal which the two regions could work towards is to forge a global consensus to launch a "Millennium Round" of multilateral trade negotiations in the year 2000.

Conclusion

I believe that East Asia will bounce back from the present crisis and resume its historic march towards economic parity with Europe and America. In the meantime, the crisis has thrown up many new investment opportunities for European business. East Asia and Western Europe are two poles in a tripolar economic world. The two regions can cooperate in many areas to their mutual advantage and to the benefit of the world economy.

(*Article written for "Trade Route Asia–Pacific", May 1999 issue, published by Stroudgate Australasia P/L.*)

The Importance of Cultural Exchange and Cooperation between Asia and Europe

Mr Co-chairman, Excellencies, Ladies and Gentlemen,

I feel like a mosquito in a nudist camp. I know what I am supposed to do but I am not sure where to begin.

I have listened attentively to the statements, questions and comments which were made yesterday and today. I would like to share with you a number of points of convergence which emerged from our discussion.

First, we all agree on the importance of culture to individuals, to countries, to the relations between countries. Culture enriches the lives of individuals. Men and women do not live by bread and rice alone. We need to nourish our minds, our spirits and our souls. Culture is also a means of uniting the human family. Cultural expressions such as music, literature, theatre, dance, painting, opera, film can easily cross boundaries of race, language, religion and ideology. In this way, culture is a tremendous force which can break down barriers of prejudice and ignorance and contribute to the ideal of an international civil society.

Second, we all agree on the importance of building a new bridge linking the New Europe and the New Asia. For this bridge to be strong, it must rest on several pillars. One such pillar is culture. Asia and Europe are the homes of several ancient, rich and vibrant cultures. There is much that we can offer each other. There is also much that we can do together, for the further development of our own cultures and for the creation of a third culture which would draw inspiration from Asian as well as European cultures.

Third, cultural cooperation and exchange between Asia and Europe should take three forms:

- the exchange of finished products;
- the exchange of techniques or forms; and
- the sharing of the creative process.

All three forms of exchange are important. However, for young artists, the sharing of the creative process is the most inspiring.

Fourth, cultural cooperation and exchange between Asia and Europe should not focus exclusively on antiquities, the exotic, and what is politically safe. It is important to include in such exchanges contemporary art and contemporary theatre. To make this possible, we need to strengthen the culture of tolerance and the acceptance of diversity.

Fifth, it was remarked that Asians generally know more about Europe than Europeans do about Asia. It is desirable to narrow this gap. The key is education and we should start with the young. European students should be exposed at an early age to Asian languages and cultures. The wisdom is that knowledge leads to understanding and understanding leads to respect.

Sixth, European impressarios, directors of festivals, museums, galleries and performing arts centres are often not well informed about what Asia has to offer. It is necessary to close this gap. I am happy to announce that ASEF and the Visiting Arts of the UK will be co-organising a conference in London from 1 to 4 April to bring together those from Europe who have an interest in presenting Asian arts and those from Asia who have exportable cultural products. We will be bringing five participants from each ASEM country.

Seventh, we had a good discussion on the roles of the government, business, foundations and high-net-worth individuals in supporting the arts and cultural exchange. We acknowledge that we are living in an era when governments are being downsized, when many governments are faced with budgetary constraints, and when the trend is to rely more on the market. The consensus at our discussion is that the government has an indispensable role to play in supporting the arts and cultural exchange. It cannot abdicate its role completely to the market. However, we need to create a partnership between the arts, governments, the business community, foundations and high-net-worth individuals.

Eighth, we recognised the growing importance of television, film, the Internet, multimedia and other new technologies. We should harness the power of the new technologies, especially the Internet and new digital technology. We should agree, at this forum, that we, the arts institutions, museums and international organisations, will put our information and directories on the Internet and on CD-ROM. In this connection, I am pleased to inform you that it is one ambition of ASEF to serve as the clearing house of all information on the relationship between Asia and Europe. We already have a website, and are in the process of recruiting a web-master. We will put on our website an inventory of arts institutions, foundations, programmes for artists-in-residence and so on.

I will now turn to the work of the four working groups. We have heard the reports on their work by the chairmen and rapporteurs. I will not attempt to summarise their conclusions. The texts of the reports of the four working groups will be published as part of the report of this forum.

I will now come to the most difficult part of my summation. You will recall that at the beginning of our forum yesterday, the two co-chairmen said that we want the forum to have three deliverables:

- To begin the process of building networks between Asian and European cultural workers;
- To press on with the ongoing task of drawing up an inventory of the cultural exchanges between Europe and Asia; and
- To identify five or six cogent, important, and new projects which can be implemented.

To pick a few projects from the many which emerged from the working groups is an invidious task. I must therefore apologise for the inevitable arbitrariness with which choices had to be made. I commend the following projects to you.

First, we should support the proposal of the Government of Denmark to host a major show of contemporary Asian art in the autumn of 1999. There is considerable scepticism in the West concerning contemporary Asian art. The latter is often viewed as lacking originality, as being derivative. We believe that this perception is mistaken. We believe that there are artists in Asia who are creating outstanding works which are modern but not Western, which are rooted in local tradition but not entombed in such tradition. Obviously, the choice of the curator is critical.

Second, Finland has proposed a project in the world of film for the year 2000. In that year, Helsinki and eight other cities have been designated as some of the cultural capitals of Europe. Finland should tap the expertise of Cannes, Venice and Berlin, and invite to Helsinki six to eight of Asia's most brilliant young film-makers. There will be a festival of their best films which will also be shown in the other seven cultural capitals. It would be wonderful if, in the same year, a country in Asia would take the lead by inviting the best young film-makers of Europe to visit Asia and to have their films shown in Tokyo, Hong Kong, Singapore, Shanghai, Pusan and other Asian cities.

Third, given the pervasive influence of television, I am pleased to inform the meeting that my co-chairman, Jerome Clement, the President of Arte, is prepared to take an initiative. Arte is Europe's pre-eminent cultural television channel. Mr Clement is prepared to convene a meeting in France comprising his existing partners, as well as potential partners from Asia, to discuss the possibility of exchanging programmes, co-production and even the possibility of strategic alliances.

Fourth, a modest project that could bring long-term benefits is to organise at the next Frankfurt Book Fair a meeting of the leading book publishers of Asia and Europe. The meeting will consider ways to facilitate the flow of books published in Europe to Asia and vice versa. The meeting will also consider the commercial feasibility of translating, for example, the ten best books published each year in Europe into Asian languages and vice versa.

Fifth, in many countries in Asia, museums are in very poor condition. They are underfunded. They lack adequate numbers of curatorial experts, restorers and experts in the design and mounting of exhibitions. Europe should take the lead in helping to train Asians in such fields of expertise and, more generally, in upgrading the quality of museums in Asia. Asia also needs the help of Europe and UNESCO in preserving some of Asia's traditional performing arts that are in danger of extinction.

Sixth, by the turn of the century, the majority of the world's population will live in towns and cities. The future of our cities is therefore one of the most important challenges facing humankind. What can we do to promote sustainable cities? What can we do to promote the development of cities that strike the right harmony between nature and the built environment, between heritage and modernity, between the physical and the social environment? These are critical questions. We need to think more deeply about them and to conceptualise a conference that would seek answers to these questions, and an exhibition showing examples of good and bad urban design and buildings.

(*Concluding Remarks delivered at the Asia–Europe Cultural Forum in Paris on 6 February 1998.*)

The Importance of
Cultural Development

The Asia–Europe Foundation (ASEF) recently co-organised a conference in Beijing, with the Chinese Ministry of Culture, on the important role that cultural industries play in the development of culture. By "cultural industries" we mean the producers of cultural products, including films, music, publishing and other creative industries. The following are some of my reflections based on discussions during the conference.

First, one of the objectives of the conference was to enhance understanding of the importance of cultural development and cultural industries and the relationship between them. Why is it important for every country, Asian or European, rich or poor, to conserve, protect and develop its arts and heritage? Culture and heritage are important not just because they attract tourists, generate income and employment, but because they tell us who we are. Culture and heritage can reinforce our identity and national pride. No country can call itself developed if it does not have a culture-loving people. The current rankings of countries by GDP, by economic and social indicators, are all unsatisfactory because they do not include any cultural indicators. We need a new index ranking countries based on the quality of life, which, in addition to economic and social indicators, would also include cultural and environmental indicators.

Second, an important theme of the conference was the impact of globalisation on culture and the arts. Some participants expressed the fear that globalisation may lead to the emergence of a boring, homogeneous world culture. Other participants, especially Asians, expressed fear that with globalisation, Asian traditional arts and heritage may be condemned to an inevitable decline. I do not agree with either view. I believe that globalisation will lead to a more multicultural world. One manifestation of this trend is the new interest in world music. There are many opportunities for the music industry and Asian musicians to exploit this trend. Europeans are increasingly open to and interested in Asian arts and culture. The quality of Asian cultural products must, however, be high. Let me cite an example. The Japan Foundation and TheatreWorks of Singapore recently co-produced a multicultural Asian production of "Lear". The cast included a Japanese Noh actor, a Peking Opera star, a dance from Thailand, actors, dancers and singers from Malaysia, Indonesia and Singapore. The Director and composer were from Singapore. The show was a hit in Japan, Hong Kong, Singapore, Indonesia and Australia. It will be performed this summer in Berlin and Copenhagen.

Asian traditional arts and culture will have a bright future for two reasons. First, Asians are eager to rediscover their cultural roots. Local productions have a resonance with their audiences which foreign productions cannot have. Second, because Europe is ready to welcome high-quality Asian arts and culture.

Third, another theme of the conference was the worldwide trend towards the downsizing of the state or public sector and the expansion of the market. What is the impact of this trend on the development of culture and the arts? One possible consequence is that, in most countries, the support of the public sector for culture and heritage will decline. It is, however, important that this conference record a consensus that the state cannot withdraw altogether from its patronage of arts and culture. In both the building of new infrastructure as well as in the development of the software, the state must continue to play a central role. If our objective is to develop high culture and not just pop culture, the patronage of the public sector is an imperative.

However, in our new world, the patronage of the arts cannot come only from the state. It must also include the business community and high-net-worth individuals. In the UK, "Business for the Arts" gives more money to arts groups than the British government. In America, the largest source of financial support comes from wealthy individuals. In Asia, we must develop such good traditions. Governments can use tax incentives to encourage such private support for the arts. For example, in Singapore, a donor of an object or collection to a museum is given a tax benefit equivalent to 100 per cent or 200 per cent of the value of the donation.

Fourth, another worldwide trend is the expansion of the market. The impact of this trend is the growth of cultural industries, spanning the whole spectrum from publishing, music, film, television, theatre, dance to visual arts and museums. How should the artistes and arts groups view the cultural industries? Should they view them as partners or adversaries? My view is that artistes and arts organisations should regard the cultural industries as partners rather than as adversaries. Writers need agents and publishers. Arts groups, museums and galleries need corporate sponsors. Composers, musicians and singers need the music industry. Artistes and arts groups need impresarios. There is much synergy between artistes, arts groups, the public sector and the business community.

Fifth, we live in a new world. In the 21st century, the world economy will be increasingly driven by the creative industries and knowledge-intensive industries. In order for societies and economies to prosper in this new world, governments must reform their educational systems to encourage creativity, and to create an environment in which the arts and technological sciences can mingle and cross-fertilise. Governments, both in Asia and in Europe, are increasingly aware of the importance of arts and creativity in their countries' economic future. For these reasons, I am convinced that art and culture will enjoy a new renaissance in the 21st century.

(*Paper submitted to UNESCO Cultural Policies for Development Unit as editorial for webpage of 25 May 1999.*)

Towards a Constructive Dialogue on Human Rights

Introduction

I would like to congratulate France and Sweden for their joint initiative in convening this seminar on Human Rights and the Rule of Law. I wish to thank the Raoul Wallenberg Institute for organising the seminar and giving me this opportunity to share a few thoughts with you. My objective is to consider how we can steer the dialogue between Asia and Europe on human rights, which is often characterised by conflict, acrimony and misunderstanding, towards a more constructive direction.

Facts about the ASEM Family

We, the 26 members of ASEM, belong to a new family. In this family we have 16 European and 10 Asian partners. The European members of the family are bound by history, religion and culture. It is not an exaggeration to say that they share a common legal tradition and a common political culture. It is these commonalities which make it possible for them to subscribe to the European Convention of Human Rights and to establish a European Court of Justice.

The 10 Asian members of the ASEM family, unlike their European counterparts, do not share a common legal tradition and political culture. East Asia is a region of great diversity. This is why there is no Asian Convention of Human Rights or an Asian Court. Even in Southeast Asia, where a successful regional organisation, ASEAN, has existed for 30 years, the process of evolution has not reached a point where we are ready to adopt an ASEAN Convention of Human Rights. For the time being, there is not even a consensus for every ASEAN country to have a national commission on human rights and an ombudsman.

Living with Diversity

The beginning of wisdom is to recognise that the ASEM family is a diverse family. We must therefore learn to live with diversity. This is easier for Asians than for Europeans to do. Because Asia is such a diverse continent, Asians do not usually expound the view that an Asian norm should also be accepted as the universal norm. In the case of Europe, because of its greater homogeneity and because of the superiority which it has enjoyed for the last several hundred years, some European intellectuals tend to hold the view that what is good for Europe must be good for the world. This mindset must change for a constructive dialogue to begin.

The Prerequisites for a Constructive Dialogue

Mutual Respect

The first prerequisite for a constructive dialogue between Asia and Europe is for the dialogue to be conducted on the basis of mutual respect. We should be conscientious in seeking understanding. We should be slow to cast judgements on others, especially when we do not fully understand the history, culture and tradition and context of the country in question. We should also aspire to adopt an attitude of humility, believing that no country, no system, no set of values, is perfect.

From Unilateralism to Multilateralism

The second prerequisite is for the West to stop resorting to the use of unilateral action to "punish" certain Asian countries for their transgression of the human rights of their people. It seems to detract from the spirit of the rules of natural justice for a country to act as witness, prosecutor and judge. If you have a complaint against a certain country, bring that country to the appropriate multilateral forum. If there is no appropriate multilateral forum it is possible to invent a bilateral forum such as that recently agreed between President Clinton and President Jiang.

Accepting a Core of Universal Human Rights

Third, I believe that there is a core of human rights which are universal in character and from which there must be no derogation. Asians and Europeans can agree that genocide, torture, slavery, racial discrimination, discrimination against women, and the abuse of children should be universally condemned. In addition, I would urge all Asian states to accede to two international Covenants — the Covenant on Civil and Political Rights and the Covenant on Economic, Social and Cultural Rights.

Recognising Points of Divergence

Fourth, the problem is that there are points of divergence between Asia and Europe outside the core. For example, is it ever justifiable for an Asian country to infringe on the liberty of the individual in the interest of the society? Every society needs to strike an appropriate balance between, on the one hand, the rights of the individual, and, on the other hand, the rights of the community. If an Asian country decides that in order to fight the drug menace, the State should have the right to ask a citizen for a sample of his urine, should the West condemn such a practice as a violation of the individual's liberty? Is it wrong for some Asian countries to impose the death penalty on drug traffickers?

Let me cite another example. Many of the Southeast Asian countries are plural societies in which race, religion and language are potentially explosive issues. They are also relatively new and fragile nations. Given this background, is it wrong for Brunei, Indonesia, Malaysia and Singapore to have banned Salman Rushdie's book *The Satanic Verses*? Can Europe understand the different context of Southeast Asia? Can Europe ever accept that in order to preserve social harmony and public order, it is sometimes necessary for an Asian country to compromise the freedom of speech and freedom of the press.

Concept of Good Government

Fifth, not all the countries of East Asia are democracies. Democracy is in any case a means to an end. The desired goal is good government. Asians and Europeans aspire to live under good government. Is it possible to use the concept of good government as a way of reconciling Asia and Europe?

What is my concept of good government? A good government should possess the following characteristics:

1. It should be accountable to the people, preferably through a regularly held free and fair election;
2. It should be competent;
3. It should be clean and non-corrupt;
4. It should accept the rule of law and judicial independence;
5. It should treat its citizens in a humane way;
6. It should provide citizens with adequate housing, quality education, adequate employment, affordable health care, public order, social harmony and a clean environment;
7. It should foster the growth of a civil society;
8. It should behave as a responsible citizen of the world community;
9. It should establish the institution of an ombudsman; and
10. It should promote transparency in its decision-making processes.

If we build an index based upon these indicators and score the 25 ASEM governments, it would be interesting to see how they are ranked. Such an index of good government would be much more meaningful than the way in which Freedom House,

Amnesty International and other Western human rights organisations classify and rank Asian countries. It is a myth to equate democracy with good government. Churchill was closer to the truth when he said it was the least bad form of government.

Balancing Human Rights and Human Responsibilities

Sixth, 1998 marks the 50th anniversary of the Universal Declaration of Human Rights. We should celebrate the occasion. We should acknowledge the many ways in which the Declaration has made our world a safer and more humane one. It is, however, also an occasion for reflection. There are many leaders in the developing world who feel that the Universal Declaration of Human Rights represents a Western world view, and should be amended. Without detracting in any way from my commitment to the Universal Declaration of Human Rights, I wish to commend to your attention the Universal Declaration of Human Responsibilities proposed by the Inter-Action Council. The Council is chaired by Helmut Schmidt, the former German Chancellor.

What is the rationale of the Universal Declaration of Human Responsibilities? The rationale is that for every right of freedom there is a correlative obligation or responsibility. There must therefore always be a balance between freedom and responsibility. The Declaration is also an attempt to reconcile Western culture which emphasises the rights of individuals with the cultures of many Asian societies which emphasise the interests of the family, community and country.

(Speech delivered at Raoul Wallenberg Institute's Informal ASEM Seminar on Human Rights and the Rule of Law in Lund, Sweden, on 13 December 1998.)

Asian Values Reconsidered

No Asian Consensus on Asian Values

I must begin with a big caveat, which is that there is no consensus among Asian intellectuals and scholars on whether there are specifically "Asian values". Some Asians believe that there are "good" values and "bad" values but no such thing as Asian values. Those who hold this view therefore believe that values are universal in character. Others believe that because Asia is so big and heterogeneous there is no set of values which is shared by all Asians. However, those who hold this view may contend that some countries in Asia, for example, the Confucianist societies, do share a common set of values. There is a third school of thought, and this consists of those who believe that in spite of Asia's heterogeneity, Asians who live in Northeast Asia and Southeast Asia do share particular personal and social values. This school believes that there are specifically Asian values and ideals just as there are American values and ideals and European values and ideals.

Western Opposition to Asian Values

I have been puzzled by the fact that many American and European intellectuals have reacted so negatively to the concept of Asian values. For example, the former Governor of Hong Kong, and currently the European Commissioner for External Relations, Chris Patten, devoted a chapter in his book, *East and West*, to debunking Asian values. During the East Asian monetary and economic crisis of 1997 and 1998, a number of Western scholars and commentators took the opportunity to criticise Asian values. They argued that the crisis was due, in part, to the pernicious influence of Asian values. I wonder what those commentators would have to say now that the tiger economies are roaring back to life. In comparison, there is not generally a negative reaction in Asia when Americans and Europeans talk about their own respective values and ideals. Why does the West react in such a negative way when Asians profess their belief in Asian values? I think there are three possible reasons.

West Does Not Accept Asia as an Equal

First, I believe that the West has not yet come to accept Asia as an equal. The West has dominated Asia for the major part of the past two hundred years. Most people in the West, including its intellectuals, still regard Asia and Asians as inferior. For example, one eminent Western intellectual contended, in an Op-Ed essay in the *International Herald Tribune* a few years ago, that East Asia does not represent any positive values.[a] This old mindset has not changed.

A Potential Challenge to Western Hegemony

Second, I suspect that the West cannot accept the concept of Asian values because the latter could pose a challenge to Western intellectual hegemony. The truth is that we still live in a world which is politically, militarily, economically, culturally, intellectually and morally dominated by the West. Of all the regions of the non-Western world, only East Asia has the potential to achieve parity with the West. By 1996, the ten major economies of East Asia were, collectively, as large as the United

---

[a] George Hicks, "Greater China Should Think Again about Being So Different", *International Herald Tribune*, 23 November 1993. (For a response to this article, see Tommy Koh's "The 10 Values That Undergird East Asian Strength and Success", *International Herald Tribune*, 11–12 December 1993.)

States (25 per cent of the world economy) and only slightly smaller than the European Union (29 per cent). East Asia is also home to some of the world's oldest and richest civilisations. These civilisations are going through a renaissance, powered by a new generation of Asian writers, artists, musicians, dramatists, dancers, film-makers and actors. Therefore, East Asia has the potential to challenge Western domination in the economic, cultural, intellectual and moral spheres in the 21st century.

Giving Asian Values a Bad Name

Third, some of East Asia's political leaders have given Asian values a bad name by seeking to justify their abuses of power and the inequities of their societies in the name of Asian values. For example, corruption, collusion and nepotism should be condemned by all Asians. They have nothing to do with Asian values. To put it more accurately, they have everything to do with bad Asian values but nothing to do with good Asian values. This leads me to my point that it is essential to distinguish between good Asian values and bad Asian values. Not all Asian values are good values just as not all Western values are good values. There are good Asian values and bad Asian values, just as there are good Western values and bad Western values.

Defining Asian Values

Very little empirical work has been done to ascertain what personal and societal values East Asians hold in common. One of the few researchers who have tried to do so is an American, David Hitchcock, of the Center for Strategic and International Studies in Washington, D.C. In 1994, he interviewed over 100 people in Singapore, Kuala Lumpur, Jakarta, Bangkok, Shanghai, Beijing, Seoul and Tokyo. The people he interviewed were experts from research institutes, officials, businessmen and women, journalists, and cultural and religious leaders. What were the principal conclusions of Hitchcock's survey?

Hitchcock found a surprising degree of congruence between the personal and societal values of Northeast Asians and Southeast Asians. On personal values, Asians from the two sub-regions gave equal emphasis to the importance of hard work, respect for learning, honesty, self-reliance, self-discipline and the fulfilment of obligations. On societal values, the respondents agreed on the importance of an orderly society, harmony, respect for authority, official accountability and consensus.

Differences between Asian and American Values

Hitchcock's study, entitled "Asian Values and the United States, How Much Conflict?", was intended to ascertain the differences between Asian and American values. I know of no comparable study of the differences between Asian and European values. I will, however, assume that European values are closer to American values than they are to Asian values. On that assumption, let us see what were the differences which Hitchcock found between Asian and American values.

Differences of Personal Values

On personal values, Asians emphasised the importance of respect for learning, honesty and self-discipline, whereas Americans emphasised achieving success in life, personal achievement and helping others.

Differences of Societal Values

On societal values, Hitchcock identified three differences between the responses of Asians and Americans. First, 71 per cent of the Asians compared to 11 per cent of the Americans emphasised the importance of an orderly society. Second, 82 per cent of the Americans compared to 32 per cent of the Asians emphasised the importance of personal freedom. Third, 78 per cent of the Americans compared to 29 per cent of the Asians emphasised the importance of individual rights.

Differences between Asian and Western Values

Hitchcock's survey confirms my impression that there are significant differences between the personal and societal values of Asians and Americans. To recapitulate, Asians emphasise the importance of orderly society whereas Americans emphasise the importance of personal freedom and individual rights. Asians emphasise the importance of respect for learning and self-discipline whereas Americans emphasise the importance of success, personal achievement and helping others. Given the above differences, it is therefore not surprising that East Asia and the West do not always hold identical views on human rights, democracy and good governance.

The Dentsu Survey of Asian and Western Values

In 1997 and 1998, the Dentsu Institute of Human Studies of Japan carried out two surveys on personal values. In 1997, the survey sampled households in Britain, France, Germany, Sweden and the United States. In 1998, the survey sampled households in Japan, China, South Korea, Thailand, Singapore and India. The respondents were asked to evaluate the relative importance of the following nine attributes: (i) financial wealth; (ii) acquiring high quality goods; (iii) family relationships; (iv) success in work; (v) mental relaxation; (vi) leisure activity; (vii) living for the present; (viii) striving to achieve personal goals; and (ix) having good relationships with others.

Charles Wolf on Dentsu Survey

Writing in the *International Herald Tribune*, Dr Charles Wolf, Jr of the Hoover Institution and Rand Corporation, wrote that the Dentsu survey "provides convincing evidence for separating the mythology about Asian values from reality". He concluded that "Asian values are decidedly more similar to Western values than is usually presumed, and on some points Asians diverge more from one another than they do from Americans and

Western Europeans". Charles Wolf argued that the economic success of East Asia was due entirely to its sound economic policies.[b]

A Japanese Response to Wolf

I asked three colleagues with the Dentsu Institute, Shinji Fukukawa, Seiko Yamazaki and Naoko Odaka, for their comments on Charles Wolf's article. Three of their important comments are reproduced below.

There Are Asian Values

Fukukawa, Yamazaki and Odaka noted that:

> "We believe that it is important to recognise the diversity as well as the similarity among Asian nations. As found in our survey, the relative importance accorded to family and collective identity over individuality, for example, is a common trait among Asian people when compared to those in the West. Another example is the acceptance of Japanese popular culture in the Asian region. While, to be sure, these are things distinctly Japanese, people also see something they can relate to more than they can to American pop culture. In this sense, there certainly are values that can be construed as being 'Asian'."

It Is Not Just Economics

On whether culture plays any role in East Asia's good economic performance, they wrote:

> "… it is hard to imagine that economic policy alone shapes the future of the economy, because economic policies are in turn shaped by values that are derived from tradition, or changing tradition for that matter. Furthermore, if more accountability is required of politicians and bureaucrats in

---

[b]*International Herald Tribune*, 10 November 1999, p. 8.

Asian societies (as it is happening in Japan), the need to reflect public opinion and sentiment will increase. There are political regimes in Asia which differ radically from those of Western democracy. It may be harder for such regimes to reflect public opinion, but they too cannot be totally free from the influence of their traditional and national values. On this point we do not agree with Charles Wolf's argument."

Fusion of Values and Systems

I very much agree with the conclusion of Fukukawa, Yamazaki and Odaka:

"Against the backdrop of globalisation, Asian and Western States (and, of course, other States) are entering a phase of revolutionary change. We believe that by looking at the changes both in the values people embrace and the political, economic and social systems, and understanding the dynamism between the two, we will reach a better understanding of what is happening now and which direction our world is heading for."

Asian and European Perspectives on Human Rights

In November 1998, the Asia–Europe Foundation co-organised a colloquium on "Human Rights and Human Responsibilities" with the German newspaper, *Die Zeit*, in Hamburg. The colloquium brought together about 50 East Asian and West European intellectuals. The colloquium agreed that the Universal Declaration of Human Rights had helped to make the world a more humane place. However, there were two disagreements between some Asian and some European participants at the colloquium.

The first disagreement was over whether, given the diversity of the world in which we live, we could agree that "different places should be allowed to progress at different paces" towards the achievement of the universal standards. Many Asians argued that it was unrealistic to expect all countries to attain universal standards and ideals at the same time. In their view, some countries, which are starting from a lower base, should be given more time. This argument was rejected by most of the European participants.

The second disagreement was on whether, in judging the human rights situation of a country, one should take into account its history and context. Let us take China as an example. Should we judge China by the standards of, for example, contemporary Sweden or should China be judged in the context of the dramatic progress it has made since the beginning of the Deng era? A former US ambassador to China, J Stapleton-Roy, had written that no government in human history has done so much for so many people in such a short time as the present Government of China. Most European participants were not sympathetic to this point of view. They felt that neither history nor context could be used as an excuse for violations of human rights.

The Three Flaws

At the Hamburg colloquium, we agreed that our record of achievements in the field of human rights over the past 50 years contained at least three flaws. First, we acknowledged that we are all guilty of double standards. We tend to criticise states with which we have little or no national interests and which are not in a position to retaliate against us. There is an inescapable tension faced by all governments in reconciling their commitment to principles and the interests of the state.

Second, the development of international human rights law during the past 50 years has been driven by a dominant West. The views, concerns and interests of the non-Western world were often ignored or inadequately considered. A case in point is the current campaign by Europe to impose its opposition to capital punishment on the rest of the world as a new universal norm. Is it right for Europe to do so when the fact is that there are 113 countries (23 of which have not carried out the death penalty for the last 10 years) which retain capital punishment in their laws, as against 83 which have legally abolished the death penalty?

Third, because of its ignorance of the conditions in some developing countries, the good intentions of the West sometimes do more harm than good. Let me cite an example. In October 1998, I co-chaired a colloquium on labour relations at The Hague, in the Netherlands. A representative of a European non-governmental organisation told us that it had succeeded in closing down a factory in Bangladesh which employed child labour. Later, it found to its horror that because of the poverty of the families, some of the girls had been forced into prostitution. The moral of the story is that in order to wipe out child labour we need a positive agenda of poverty alleviation as well as an agenda of targeting the evil people who exploit children.

Conclusion

I want to conclude on a positive note. Because of globalisation, information technology and human mobility, we have truly become citizens of one world. We must therefore evolve a global consensus on what is good and evil and what is right and wrong. The new Asia can make important contributions towards the development of such a consensus. In our dialogue, we should be diligent in seeking understanding and be slow to judge. I like a native American saying that you should walk for at least three days in another man's moccasin before you judge him. We should avoid confrontation as much as possible. We should treat each other with respect. With such an attitude, I am confident that we will succeed in increasing our points of convergence and reducing our points of divergence.

(Article for May 2000 issue of "Asia–Pacific Review", journal of the Institute for International Policy Studies, Tokyo, Japan.)

What Can East Asia Learn from the European Union?

Introduction

Twice, in the first half of this century, Europe plunged the world into devastating wars. Seventy million people perished in the First and Second World Wars. Fifty-three years ago, Europe was in ruins. European hearts were filled with anger and bitterness. Who could have foreseen in 1945 that two generations later, historical enemies would be reconciled and Western Europe would be united, peaceful and prosperous? The European Union is nothing short of a miracle. It is for this reason that I wish to ask what lessons can East Asia learn from the European Union.

Lesson No. 1

The first lesson which East Asia can learn from the European Union is that history need not repeat itself. It is possible to put aside deep divides of language, culture, religion and centuries of conflict and war. It is possible for visionary leaders to win the hearts and minds of their peoples in order to persuade them to discard the bitter legacy of the past and to embrace the sweet promise of a better future. After the Second World War, Western Europe was blessed with a number of such leaders. Jean Monnet and Robert Schuman of France were the architects of the European Coal and Steel Community which came into existence in 1952. Paul-Henri Spaak of Belgium was the principal architect of the 1957 Treaties of Rome, which established the European

Economic Community (EEC) and the European Atomic Energy Community (EURATOM). In 1963, General Charles de Gaulle and Chancellor Konrad Adenauer signed the Franco–German Friendship Treaty. This brought about a reconciliation between two historical enemies. Another European visionary who has been vindicated by history is Paul Werner of Luxembourg who, in 1970, put forward a plan to establish an economic and monetary union.

Is East Asia prepared to learn the first lesson? The answer in Southeast Asia is definitely yes. Formed in 1967, two years after the end of Indonesia's armed confrontation against Malaysia, which then included Singapore, its members were prepared to put aside the quarrels of the past in order to build a common future. When the Cold War ended, ASEAN extended a hand of friendship to Vietnam and welcomed it into the family. The leaders of Southeast Asia are determined to achieve their common vision of one united Southeast Asia. This dream will be realised when Cambodia is admitted into the family.

The picture in Northeast Asia is less satisfactory. Historic reconciliation of the kind that occurred between England, France and Germany has not taken place between China and Japan or between Japan and Korea. The ghosts of the past continue to haunt the triangular relationship between China, Japan and Korea. It is time to exorcise the ghosts. East Asia needs visionary leaders of the calibre and stature of Monnet, Schuman, Spaak, de Gaulle, Adenauer and Werner who could simultaneously bury the past and inspire the peoples of East Asia with the vision of a New Asia.

Lesson No. 2

The second lesson which East Asia can learn from the European Union is the capacity, the ability and the willingness of the members of the Union to engage in a free and candid exchange of views no matter how controversial the issue. Such openness does not exist in East Asia, not even in ASEAN.

Let me cite an example. Last year, much of Southeast Asia was smothered for months by a thick blanket of smoke and soot caused by forest fires in Indonesia. According to the UN, about 80 per cent of the fires were started by logging companies and palm oil plantations in order to clear land. Although the actions of these companies were contrary to Indonesia's law and international environmental law and although Indonesia's neighbours suffered economic loss as well as damage to the health of their populations, ASEAN's corporate culture prevented Indonesia's neighbours from engaging her in a free and candid exchange of views. Such a situation would be unthinkable in Western Europe.

I appreciate that "face" is very important in East Asia. I acknowledge that the idea of an East Asian Community is very young. The 10 leaders of East Asia, namely, China, Japan, South Korea and the ASEAN 7 (Brunei, Indonesia, Malaysia, the Philippines, Singapore, Thailand and Vietnam) met only for the first time in December 1997 in Kuala Lumpur. The ASEAN Regional Forum (ARF), established to deal with security problems, is a mere four years old. ASEAN, however, will be 31 years old this August. It is strong and mature enough to allow a greater degree of openness in its deliberations. I do not believe that it will be shaken to its foundation if members of ASEAN were to engage in a frank but fraternal discussion of the forest fires in Indonesia. On the contrary, I believe that this would allow ASEAN to emerge as a more relevant and stronger institution. ASEAN's failure to take decisive action in the face of one of the world's worst environmental disasters has reduced its prestige and credibility in the eyes of ASEAN's own citizens and of the world.

Lesson No. 3

The third lesson which East Asia can learn from the European Union is that institutions matter. As Jean Monnet once wrote, nothing lasting can be built without institutions. The European

Union has established a number of key institutions, for example, the Council of Ministers, the European Commission, the European Parliament, the Court of Justice, the Commission on Human Rights, the European Central Bank, and many others. At every critical juncture of its history, the European Union has been able to move forward towards its goal of an ever closer union by creating or re-engineering its institutions.

The culture of East Asia is significantly different from that of Western Europe. In East Asia, leaders prefer to pursue their goals by building trust, by a process of consultation, mutual accommodation and consensus. This is sometimes referred to as the "ASEAN Way". There is a general reluctance to build institutions and to rely on rules and regulations.

The recent currency and economic crisis in East Asia has, however, shown that the "ASEAN Way" needs to be supplemented by institutions. We have no regional surveillance mechanism which could have alerted us to the seriousness of the situation. Once the crisis occurred, we had no institutions which could have mobilised our collective resources to help the economies in distress in a timely manner. Japan's initiative to establish an Asian Monetary Fund, linked to the IMF, was not properly understood and had to be aborted.

In my view, the time has come for East Asia, in general, and ASEAN in particular, to strengthen existing institutions and to build new institutions to complement the "ASEAN Way".

Conclusion

We stand on the threshold of the third millennium. The tectonic plates of the world's political economy are shifting. This is therefore a moment in history for Asian thinkers to summon the courage to think long term and to transcend the old paradigm. I believe that our current economic difficulties are temporary in nature. I believe that East Asia will rise again. I wish to inspire East Asians with the vision that in the next century and millennium East Asia can become, like Western Europe, a united, peaceful and prosperous community. In order to achieve that vision we need to bring about a historic reconciliation between China and Japan and between Japan and Korea. We also need to enmesh all the countries of Northeast and Southeast Asia in an ever closer union, of markets, of people and of our minds.

(Speech delivered at the Foreign Correspondents Club of Hong Kong on 9 July 1998. An edited version of this speech was published in the International Herald Tribune *on 10 July 1998.)*

CRISIS AND CHANGE WITHIN ASIA AND EUROPE
Implications for Asia–Europe Relations

Asia's economic crisis was a test-case for its relations with Europe. Contrary to popular perceptions at the time, Europe did contribute substantially to Asia's recovery, thus laying the foundations for a strong relationship in the future.

The Second Asia–Europe Rendezvous in London

Introduction

The second summit meeting between the 16 leaders of the European Union and the 10 leaders of East Asia will take place in London on 3–4 April 1998. This is therefore an opportune moment for us to discuss the following questions:

- Has Europe lost its interest in East Asia in view of the recent economic turmoil in this region?
- What has the Asia–Europe Meeting (ASEM) process achieved since the first Summit in March 1996?
- What are the deliverables of the London Summit?

Has Europe Lost Interest in East Asia?

I believe that Europe has not lost its interest in East Asia. I am confident that Europe will prove to Asia that it is not a fair-weather friend. On the contrary, Europe will live up to the maxim that "a friend in need is a friend indeed".

Why am I so confident?

First, I expect all 16 European leaders to attend the London Summit.

Second, the recent turmoil in East Asia does not and cannot erase certain economic trends and developments of the last several decades. East Asia's share of the world economy has been steadily increasing from 9 per cent in 1965, to 15 per cent in 1975, to 24 per cent in 1993. Europe has major financial and economic interests in East Asia. In 1996, the EU exported US$123 billion of goods and services to East Asia, more than the US. Indeed, East Asia has supplanted the US as the largest export market for the EU.

Third, we live in a world dominated by three centres of economic, political, and cultural power: the US, Europe and East Asia. We can describe it as "the romance of the three kingdoms". The challenge is to ensure that the three "kingdoms" are friendly and open to one another. Others have described the challenge as ensuring that the three sides of the triangle are strong and balanced.

The point I want to make here is that ASEM is not at the expense of Europe's transatlantic ties or East Asia's transpacific ties. The US should therefore not view ASEM as a threat but as an asset which could contribute to our shared goal of building a more stable and prosperous world.

What Has ASEM Achieved since Bangkok?

ASEM is obviously an idea whose time has come. In the two years since the Bangkok Summit, over 30 meetings, events and projects have been implemented.

ASEM has a unique character which differentiates it from APEC and various transatlantic organisations such as NATO and the OSCE. Unlike those institutions, ASEM has a very broad agenda, which seeks to build bridges between not only our political leaders and officials but also between our business communities and our civil societies.

During the past two years, our foreign ministers have initiated a political dialogue; our economic and finance ministers as well as our senior trade officials have met; the Asia–Europe Business Forum has met twice, and a Business Conference has been held; 106 young leaders from the two regions had a fruitful meeting in Japan; the representatives of our universities have met twice; and there have been various other meetings on science and technology, on customs cooperation, on the financing of infrastructural projects, on environmental technology, and on television journalism.

I hope you will forgive me if I make a brief reference to the Asia–Europe Foundation (ASEF). ASEF is the first institution to be established by ASEM. ASEF was conceived in Bangkok on 1 March 1996 and born in Singapore on 15 February 1997. Although it is only one year old, it has been a precocious baby. It has already implemented 15 projects, including helping Japan to co-organise the first Asia–Europe Young Leaders' Symposium; the Editors' Roundtable in Luxembourg; co-organising with France the first Asia–Europe Cultural Forum in Paris; inaugurating the Asia–Europe Lectures with President Jacques Santer and Prime Minister Anand Panyarachun as the first two lecturers; co-organising the first Asia–Europe Forum with a German foundation and a Singapore think-tank; launching an ASEF website; and co-organising with the UK an ambitious programme of intellectual, cultural and artistic events in London. The mandate of ASEF is to enhance better mutual understanding between Asia and Europe through greater intellectual, cultural and people-to-people exchanges.

What Are the Deliverables of the London Summit?

The London Summit will not be just a talkfest or another photo opportunity. I believe that there will be tangible and important deliverables. Let me mention a few of them.

First, I expect the leaders to issue an important statement on the East Asian economic crisis. I expect the statement to contain, *inter alia*, the following elements:

> Europe has a major stake in the economies of East Asia. For example, European banks have a combined exposure of US$350 billion, which is greater than that of the US and Japan combined;
>
> Europe has been helping the affected economies through its 30 per cent share of the IMF, as well as through additional bilateral assistance to Korea, and through the World Bank and the Asian Development Bank;

The IMF has a critical and indispensable role in restoring domestic and international confidence and the affected economies should institute the IMF prescribed programmes of reform and restructuring;

The role of IMF should be supplemented by humanitarian aid for people in distress and by export credit in order to enable commerce to flow; and

European leaders will express their confidence that East Asia will bounce back and, with the requisite reform and restructuring in place, it will emerge stronger and more competitive from the crisis.

Such a statement will be welcomed in Asia.

Second, the British have proposed two initiatives which are likely to be endorsed by the Summit. The first is to create an ASEM Trust Fund at the World Bank to provide assistance to ASEM countries, primarily in assessing the poverty impact of the crisis. The second initiative is to create a Centre on Financial Restructuring. The objective of the Centre is to help countries in their financial restructuring by providing training, advice and consultancy.

Third, the Summit will endorse an Investment Promotion Action Plan and the Trade Facilitation Action Plan. At this critical time, Asia needs a new wave of foreign direct investment from Europe. Investment missions from Europe would be very welcome. In the next several years, Asia's exports to Europe will increase significantly. It is important for Europe to keep its markets open and to combat any domestic protectionist pressures. At the same time, there must be no retreat on the part of Asia from its commitment to trade and investment liberalisation. Asian and European leaders should pledge their commitment to strengthen the WTO and to pursue the further liberalisation of trade within the multilateral framework.

Fourth, the British Prime Minister is very keen to make increased education exchange between Asia and Europe one of the highlights of the London Summit. The British have proposed a project of launching a website targeted at young people in vocational colleges. Malaysia has proposed establishing the Asia–Europe Centre at the University of Malaya. The idea of establishing educational hubs in various countries which would welcome exchange students from the other regions is likely to gather support.

Fifth, Europe has put forward an environmental initiative, linked to the European Commission's Humanitarian Office. The idea is to launch a programme in Southeast Asia to help the region cope with environmental disasters. This initiative is very timely and will be welcomed. The first priority of the programme should focus on forest fires.

Sixth, the Summit will commission a group of wise men and women, to be known as the Asia–Europe Vision Group, to develop a medium- to long-term vision to help guide ASEM into the 21st century. The Group will submit its report to the ASEM foreign ministers in 1999 and, through them, to ASEM III in the year 2000.

Seventh, the Summit will adopt an Asia–Europe Cooperation Framework to guide, focus and coordinate ASEM activities in the period up to ASEM III. This is desirable in order to impose some sense of coherence, priority and coordination on a process which is bursting with energy and new initiatives.

Conclusion

Let me conclude by praising the British Government, in general, and the British Prime Minister Tony Blair in particular, for their outstanding job in preparing for the London Summit. With Prime Minister Blair in the chair, we are confident that our rendezvous in London will be substantive, productive and future-oriented.

(*Speech given at the Foreign Correspondents Association, Singapore, on 27 March 1998.*)

The East Asian Economic Crisis
Lessons Learnt and Prospects for Recovery

Introduction

Namaste, Your Excellencies, Mrs Colette Mathur, Dr Isher Judge Ahluwalia, friends, ladies and gentlemen,

I would like to begin by garlanding a number of institutions and individuals. I would like to offer a garland to the Government of India for inviting me to deliver this lecture. I would also like to offer a garland to the Research and Information System for the Non-Aligned and Other Developing Countries (RIS) and the Confederation of Indian Industries (CII) for co-organising this lecture. Finally, I would like to offer a special garland to my good friend and guru, Brajesh Mishra, for chairing this lecture. My friendship with Brajesh goes back 30 years to 1968. In that year I was appointed Singapore's Ambassador to the UN in New York. I was only 30 years old. I had no prior diplomatic experience. I was young, innocent and ignorant. I shall always be grateful to GP Parthasarathi, Brajesh Mishra and Alfred Gonsalves for mentoring me. This is why I have always called Brajesh my guru. I would also like to acknowledge my gratitude to Samar Sen, Rikhi Jaipal, Shankar Bajpai, Ambassador Ranganathan and others. I would not have succeeded in chairing the negotiations at the Earth Summit if not for the support and guidance of my good friend Kamal Nath.

My Affinity with Indian Culture

As a Singaporean, I feel very much at home in India. More than five per cent of our population are from the Indian subcontinent. Tamil is one of our four official languages. At school, university and in my adult careers, some of my best friends have been Indians. Gandhi and Nehru were two of my childhood heroes. I grew up in an environment in which Hinduism, Indian music and dance, the *Ramayana* and the *Mahabharata* were part of my cultural upbringing. My special affinity for Indian culture may also have been due to the fact that in my youth I had a Bengali girlfriend. She was very westernised and knew little about Bengali culture. I introduced her to the poetry of Tagore and the movies of Satyajit Ray. I took her to performances of Indian music and dance. Her mother was very impressed and liked me. Unfortunately, the daughter was less impressed and married a Caucasian man! Last year, the Indian Fine Arts Society of Singapore gave me an award. The award is called, in Tamil, "Jewel of the Art". I had been hoping that after receiving the award, my wife would start calling me her "jewel". In spite of several subtle hints it has not worked!

From Thai Crisis to Crisis of Global Capitalism

Let me now turn to the topic of my lecture. During the past sixteen months, East Asia has been faced with its worst economic crisis in three decades. What started out as a Thai crisis soon transformed from the "*tomyam*" effect (as opposed to the tequila effect) into a Southeast Asian crisis. The contagion spread to South Korea. Coincidentally, Japan is also in recession. The East Asian economic crisis was not foreseen by any one within or outside the region. It has proved to be deeper and more pervasive than anyone could have imagined. More recently, the Asian crisis has also spread to Russia and Brazil. What started out as an East Asian crisis has become a crisis of global capitalism. The collapse of Long-term Capital Management (LTCM), which led the Federal Reserve Bank to intervene, has shown that even the United States is vulnerable. For this reason, Prime Minister Tony Blair recently called for an overhaul of the international financial system and the building of a "new Bretton Woods for the next millennium".

A Hurricane which Struck without Warning

For over two decades, the countries of East Asia had been achieving annual rates of economic growth of between 6 and 10 per cent. Poverty had either been eliminated or drastically reduced. Literacy went up and infant mortality went down. The performance was so impressive that the World Bank published a report on eight of the countries with the title "The East Asian Economic Miracle". I am afraid that our success and the adulation we had received intoxicated some of our leaders. We suffered from the sin of "hubris".

When the peso crisis occurred in Mexico in 1994–1995, the consensus in East Asia was that it could not happen in our region. We had good reasons to distinguish the two situations. Mexico and the other affected Latin American countries suffered from huge government budget deficits. They had negative current account balances. They had little foreign exchange reserves. They had low savings rates. In contrast, most of the countries of East Asia enjoyed high savings, budget surpluses, and varying amounts of foreign exchange reserves. Government profligacy, which brought Latin America down, was not a sin in East Asia.

The Beginning of the Crisis

The crisis began in Thailand. Let us therefore try to understand the causes of that crisis. In my view, Thailand made four mistakes. First, it aligned the Thai baht too closely to the US dollar. As a result, the baht appreciated along with the US dollar. This led Thailand to lose its export competitiveness. Second, when Thailand liberalised its financial sector, Thai companies were able to borrow US dollars at lower interest than that for the baht. Because the Thai economy was booming, the country was flooded with foreign money. The Thai Central Bank had not kept an eye on the mounting private sector debt which, in total, exceeded Thailand's foreign exchange reserves. Third, there was misallocation of capital. Too much of the capital went into real estate and the stock exchange. As a result, Thailand developed an asset bubble. Fourth, Thailand's banks and finance companies were weak and were not properly supervised and regulated.

The Thai asset bubble was pricked and it burst. The international financial market decided to attack the baht. The Bank of Thailand tried in vain to defend the baht. After spending US$20 billion, the central bank gave up the fight and allowed the baht to float. It sank and went from 25 baht:US$1 to 42 baht:US$1. The Thai stock exchange also collapsed. The discredited government was forced to resign. A new government, headed by Prime Minister Chuan Leekpai, a leader reputed for his honesty, and backed by a team of highly competent technocrats, has taken over power.

The *Tomyam* Effect on Malaysia

In 1996 Malaysia achieved a growth rate of eight per cent. Prospects for 1997 looked promising. However, once the international market succeeded in attacking Thailand it started to probe Thailand's neighbours to ascertain their weaknesses. Malaysia had some of the problems of the Thai economy. Malaysia had a huge private sector debt. Its current account was in deficit. There was too much investment in the real estate sector and in the stock market. An asset bubble was building up. On 8 July 1997, the Malaysian ringgit came under attack. On 14 July 1997, the Central Bank of Malaysia gave up trying to defend it. The ringgit depreciated from RM2.5:US$1 to RM3.9:US$1. The Malaysian stock market lost fifty per cent of its value.

Will Capital Control Work?

On 1 September 1998, Prime Minister Mahathir dismissed his deputy and finance minister, Anwar Ibrahim, and assumed the portfolio of finance minister in addition to his other portfolios. Malaysia has imposed foreign exchange controls including a rule stipulating a minimum of one year before short-term capital brought into Malaysia can be repatriated from it. The official exchange rate has been fixed at RM3.8:US$1. It is too early to say whether Malaysia's use of capital control will work. Some eminent economists, such as Paul Krugman of MIT, have argued that it could work as a short-term emergency measure provided that the scheme is implemented in an honest manner and provided that the respite is used to undertake the necessary reform and restructuring and not to bail out the cronies. In the meantime, interest rates in Malaysia have come down and there is a new buoyancy in the stock exchange.

Attack on the Philippines

The next country to come under attack by the international market was the Philippines. The peso had been trading at about 25 peso to one US dollar. The Philippines had been under the tutelage of the IMF for many decades. Because of this fact, the financial system of the Philippines was generally regarded by the market as being stronger than the systems of Thailand and Indonesia. During his six years as president of the Philippines, Fidel Ramos had succeeded in turning the economy of his country around. Notwithstanding the above, the peso came under attack. On 11 July 1997, the Central Bank of the Philippines gave up the defence of the peso. It has since depreciated from 25 peso:US$1 to 39 peso:US$1.

Crisis in Indonesia

Under the 32-year rule of President Suharto, Indonesia had made tremendous progress. The economy was transformed from one dependent on the export of oil to a more diversified economy. People had access to jobs, education, health care and, via satellite television, the outside world. Suharto had also succeeded in forging a sense of Indonesian nationhood, uniting over three hundred different ethnic groups. The UN gave him awards for his achievements in family planning and poverty alleviation. His tragedy was not knowing when to step down.

When the Indonesian rupiah came under attack in August 1997, the economic crisis became inseparably linked to a political crisis. On 11 August 1997, the rupiah was trading at around 2000 rupiah:US$1. At the height of the crisis, it plummeted to 16,000 rupiah:US$1. It has since stabilised at around 8,000 rupiah:US$1. President Suharto lost his Mandate of Heaven and was forced to resign. His Vice-President, BJ Habibie, has succeeded him as president. In May 1998, serious rioting, looting, arson and the rape of ethnic Chinese women took place. These events have traumatised the Chinese community in Indonesia. One of the challenges of the post-Suharto Indonesia is to regain the confidence of the Indonesian Chinese and to assure them that the past discriminations against them will be abolished.

In the meantime, the Indonesian economy faces many challenges. Ways must be found to help the good companies of Indonesia to gain access to working capital and trade credit. Unemployment and the shortage of food have created an explosive situation. The international community and Indonesia's neighbours must join hands to bring humanitarian assistance to the people in distress.

Repeated Attacks on Hong Kong

In October 1997, repeated attacks were made by the market to break the Hong Kong dollar's peg to the US dollar. The attempts were unsuccessful. In order to defend the peg, the Hong Kong Government had to raise interest rates. High interest rates combined with an increasingly negative market sentiment caused the Hong Kong Stock Exchange to lose 50 per cent of its value.

More recently, the Hong Kong Government took two controversial actions. First, it intervened in the foreign exchange market in order to defend the peg. Second, it intervened in the stock market to buy the stock of blue chip companies. The latter action has been very controversial. Free marketers, such as Milton Friedman, who used to point to Hong Kong as the paradigm case of a capitalist economy, have criticised the Hong Kong Government as "interventionist". Other economists have, however, defended the action of the Hong Kong Government on the grounds that the attack on the Hong Kong Stock Exchange by speculators was not based on any economic fundamentals but greed. Faced with such a situation, the Hong Kong government felt that it had no choice but to teach the speculators a lesson. We have to wait and see whether the speculators have learnt their lesson or whether they will mount an even bigger attack the next time.

The World's Eleventh Largest Economy

The Republic of Korea is the eleventh largest economy in the world. The OECD has only two Asian members, Japan and South Korea. Once described as a basket case, South Korea has emerged in the past thirty years as an industrial power house. I must confess that I was not aware of Korea's economic shortcomings. What were the problems? First, the Korean conglomerates or *chaebols* were over-leveraged. Second, there was an incestuous relationship between the government, the *chaebols* and the banks. The *chaebols* were therefore able to obtain funds from the banks irrespective of the returns on such investment. The international rating agencies should have raised the red flag in 1996 because 20 of the 30 largest *chaebols* had rates of return below the cost of capital.

In November 1997, the market's sentiment on South Korea became negative. The market attacked the Korean won. It has since depreciated from 900 won:US$1 to 1400 won:US$1. On 21 November 1997, South Korea sought the IMF's help. The government of President Kim Young Sam was so discredited by the crisis that the candidate of the ruling party lost the election to Kim Dae Jung, a politician who had spent his entire life in lonely opposition. President Kim Dae Jung is the right leader to lead Korea out of the crisis because he is honest and competent and because he carries no baggage from the past.

Singapore and Taiwan

Singapore and Taiwan have survived the storm better than the other regional economies because of their sound financial institutions. Taiwan's New Taiwan dollar has depreciated by less than 20 per cent. It is still hoping to achieve a growth rate of five per cent for 1998.

Unlike Taiwan, Singapore lies in the heart of Southeast Asia. The Singapore economy has extensive trade and investment linkages to all the ASEAN countries, especially to Malaysia and Indonesia. The Singapore dollar has depreciated from S$1.5:US$1 to S$1.72:US$1. The Singapore economy is technically in recession although the economy is still expected to grow by between 0.5 to 1.5 per cent in 1998.

The Chinese Dragon Roars On

Life is full of surprises. Who could have imagined a year ago that China would have the most stable and strongest economy in East Asia? Because the Chinese yuan is still not fully convertible it has been shielded from the turmoil of the foreign exchange market. There is much speculation among economists and by the market on whether China will devalue the yuan and, if so, when. I hold a contrarian view on this question. I do not believe that the devaluation of the yuan is inevitable. Why? Because China's exports are still growing although by a smaller percentage than in the previous year. Also, because China is getting so much praise from the region and from the West for not devaluing its currency. I believe that in spite of the crisis in the region, China may still achieve its target of seven per cent growth for 1998 with low inflation. Finally, I think China knows that the devaluation of the yuan will undermine the Hong Kong dollar's peg to the US dollar. For all these reasons I therefore do not expect China to devalue the yuan in the foreseeable future.

The Enigma of Japan

My survey of the region will not be complete if I do not refer to Japan. Japan is the world's second largest economy. Japan alone accounts for about 75 per cent of East Asia's GNP. At a time when East Asia was going through a crisis, the region needed a strong, prosperous and outward-looking Japan. East Asians hoped that Japan could play a role similar to that of the United States in pulling Mexico and the other countries of Latin America out of the 1994–1995 crisis.

Japan has been unable to play such a role because it is in recession. Why is Japan in recession? First, because the Japanese banking system is in a precarious state. This is due to the fact that when the asset bubble burst eight years ago, many Japanese banks were saddled with a serious problem of non-performing loans. It took eight years before the ruling LDP and the opposition parties could agree on a US$150 billion plan to solve the problem. Second, last year former Prime Minister Hashimoto misjudged the situation and increased the consumption tax. Third, the Japanese people are not optimistic about their future. They are therefore saving instead of spending. The Obuchi government has announced a stimulus package of US$200 billion.

My criticisms of Japan should, however, be balanced by my praise for Japan. I wish to praise it for three reasons. First, Japan has contributed more to the IMF rescue packages for Thailand, Indonesia and Korea than any other country. Second, Japan proposed the establishment of a US$100 billion Asian Monetary Fund to help Asian countries in financial distress. The idea was killed by opposition from the United States and the

IMF. Third, Japan recently announced a US$30 billion Miyazawa Plan to help Southeast Asia. At the recent APEC Summit in Kuala Lumpur, Japan and the United States jointly announced a US$10 billion initiative to help affected Asian economies.

Lessons Learnt

What lessons have I learnt from the crisis?

First, I have learnt that globalisation is not just a concept but a reality. There is a world capital market. The daily transactions of the foreign exchange market are in the region of US$1.5 trillion! Money moves at the speed of a digital signal in search of profit. The movement of capital into and out of countries and regions is partly dictated by economic data and partly by sentiment. When East Asia was booming it was flooded with money. The moment confidence was lost, the funds were withdrawn. In the course of the 12 months following the Thai crisis it has been estimated that US$400 billion of portfolio investment left the region. Is there anything which can be done to moderate such volatility? Every one recognises that it is a problem but no one has come up with a solution which is internationally acceptable.

Second, the governments of East Asia failed to monitor the foreign debt of their corporate sector. It is dangerous for such foreign debt to exceed the country's foreign exchange reserves. Many companies in East Asia also made the mistake of borrowing short-term to finance long-term projects.

Third, there were serious misallocations of capital and resources. Too much money was pumped into real estate and the stock market. As a result, we had asset bubbles all over East Asia. East Asia must learn to make more efficient use of capital and resources.

Fourth, some of the seemingly profitable companies and conglomerates were profitable not because they were great companies but because they enjoyed monopolies, special preferences and privileges and access to capital on non-commercial terms.

This phenomenon has been referred to as "crony capitalism". East Asia must change its political culture and abolish all such incestuous relationships.

Fifth, several Asian countries, such as Thailand, made the mistake of aligning their currencies too closely to the US dollar. It is preferable for Asian governments to manage their currencies against a trade-weighted basket of currencies including the US dollar, the yen, the euro, and other currencies. In this context, I welcome the coming birth of the euro and hope that it will become a strong currency.

Sixth, I think some Asian countries move too rapidly in liberalising their capital account. Countries should prepare themselves before making the transition. They should first pursue sound macroeconomic and fiscal policies. They should strengthen their banks and other financial institutions and follow international best practice. They should also have a proper system of supervision and regulation and insulate the regulators from political interference. Finally, they should embrace the concept of good corporate governance, including transparency and accountability.

Will East Asia Recover?

I have no doubt that East Asia will recover. The region still enjoys some strong fundamentals, such as a strong work ethic, high savings rates, commitment to education and training, belief in free trade and pro-growth policies. If East Asia can discard its flaws and mistakes and have the courage to undertake the necessary reform and restructuring, it will bounce back leaner and more competitive than before the crisis.

I already see some light at the end of the tunnel. Let me conclude by sharing with you some good news on Korea and Thailand. This year, Korea's exports, in volume terms, have increased by 30 per cent compared with last year. Thailand's exports have increased by 15 per cent. As a result, their current accounts have moved into surplus. This has, in turn, stabilised their currencies and allowed for a reduction in their interest rates. New money is also flowing into those economies. For the period January to June 1998, Thailand received US$3 billion of foreign direct investment (FDI), which is an increase of 100 per cent over the same period in 1997. In Korea, for the period January to August 1998, the FDI was US$2.7 billion, representing an increase of 36 per cent over the same period in 1997.

I have confidence in the future of East Asia. If you share my assessment, this is an excellent time for Indian corporations to invest in East Asia and to position themselves to catch the next wave of growth there.

(*The Seventh India–ASEAN Eminent Persons Lecture delivered in New Delhi on 26 November 1998.*)

Is Asean Dead or Alive?

Introduction

The world has the impression that ASEAN is a divided, ineffective and, perhaps, even a dying organisation. What has created this impression? It has been caused by three things. First, by the perception that ASEAN has not played an effective role in responding to the worst economic crisis to hit the region in thirty years. Second, by the public display of disagreement within the family when, in July 1998, the foreign minister of Thailand, Surin Pitsuwan, supported by the foreign minister of the Philippines, Domingo Siazon, argued that the principle of non-interference in the internal affairs of other countries should be replaced by a new doctrine of constructive engagement. The other foreign ministers did not agree with this view. The world does not seem to be impressed by the fact that the ASEAN ministers arrived at a compromise, to maintain the principle of non-interference but to allow "enhanced interaction" among members of the family. Third, apart from the economic crisis, we have also seen in recent months bilateral frictions between Malaysia and Singapore; between Malaysia and Indonesia; and between Malaysia and the Philippines.

ASEAN'S Three Crises

It is always helpful to view the present from the perspective of the past and the future. In its thirty-one years of existence, ASEAN has confronted three crises.

The First Crisis

The first crisis occurred in December 1978 when Vietnam invaded and occupied Cambodia. The ASEAN family was split on the issue. Some members of the family welcomed Vietnam's action in removing the odious regime in Phnom Penh. Others, especially Thailand, questioned Vietnam's motive and objective. They felt that under the guise of humanitarian intervention Vietnam was seeking to create an Indochina federation under its hegemony. In the end, the family agreed to rally around the frontline state, Thailand, and to oppose Vietnam's invasion and occupation of Cambodia. ASEAN staged a successful diplomatic campaign which culminated in the 1991 Paris Agreement.

The Second Crisis

ASEAN faced its second crisis when the Cold War ended. Many Western scholars mistakenly thought that ASEAN was a creature of the Cold War. They argued that with the end of the Cold War and the resolution of the Cambodian conflict, ASEAN had lost its *raison d'être* and would wither away. When the Cold War ended ASEAN extended its hand of friendship to Vietnam and ended the Cold War in Southeast Asia. Since 1991, ASEAN has successfully launched three bold initiatives: (a) the ASEAN Free Trade Area (AFTA); (b) the ASEAN Regional Forum (ARF); and (c) the Asia–Europe Meeting process (ASEM). Therefore, instead of withering away with the end of the Cold War, ASEAN has embraced a new agenda and been energised by a new vigour.

The Third Crisis

ASEAN is today faced with its third crisis. This crisis has two components. The first component is the monetary and economic crisis which has plunged most of ASEAN's economies into recession. The second component consists of the bilateral strains which I referred to earlier. ASEAN's prestige has fallen to a new low. ASEAN's leaders knew that ASEAN was on trial at the recently-held summit in Hanoi.

Hanoi Summit: Success or Failure?

Was the Hanoi Summit a success or a failure? I would argue that the Hanoi Summit was a success for the following reasons.

ASEAN United

First, the leaders of ASEAN succeeded in putting aside their differences and agreed to forge a new sense of unity in Hanoi. They knew that the stake was too high and the summit must not fail. The picture of the nine ASEAN leaders linking arms was not just a public relations gesture. It was to celebrate their three concrete achievements: the Hanoi Declaration, the Hanoi Plan of Action; and the Statement of Bold Initiatives.

Need to Put Our Houses in Order

Second, the ASEAN leaders in Hanoi were not in a denial mode. They readily admitted that they had made policy mistakes. They acknowledged that some of their institutions, both in the public and private sectors, needed reform and restructuring. They accepted their responsibility to put their houses in order so that confidence would return, investments would flow back to the region and growth would resume. For example, they agreed to adopt and implement sound international financial practices and standards for their financial systems and adopt higher benchmarks for disclosure and dissemination of information.

The ASEAN leaders declared in paragraph 6 of the Hanoi Declaration:

> "We are committed to accelerating the economic and financial reforms to strengthen our respective economies. We believe that reform efforts at the national level must be reinforced by corresponding reforms at the global level to

address weaknesses in the international financial architecture and welcome the contribution of the G22 in this area."

No Retreat from Free Trade and Investment Liberalisation

Third, ASEAN did not backtrack from its commitment to free trade and investment liberalisation. On the contrary, in order to send a signal to the world, especially to the foreign investors, ASEAN leaders agreed to advance the implementation of AFTA from 2003 to 2002. They also agreed to expand the negotiations on liberalisation of services beyond the seven agreed areas.

They pledged to open up their manufacturing sectors to all foreign investors whose projects are approved by any ASEAN country between 1 January 1999 and 31 December 2000. These investors will be granted special incentives. They also agreed to open up all industries, except for a few sensitive areas, to ASEAN investors by 2003 instead of 2010.

Helping One Another

Fourth, the ASEAN leaders reaffirmed their determination to help one another. As Thai Prime Minister Chuan Leekpai, said in Hanoi, when your neighbour's house is on fire, you try to help him to put out the fire instead of trying to build a firewall around your house. ASEAN countries which could afford it had contributed varying amounts to the IMF rescue packages for Thailand and Indonesia. In Hanoi, Prime Minister Goh Chok Tong of Singapore announced a new S$12 million scholarship scheme to bring 30 ASEAN scholars to study at Singapore's universities without bond. The leaders also agreed to do a study to develop an ASEAN Information Infrastructure linking the various systems in the ASEAN countries.

Need for Rules and Institutions

Fifth, ASEAN's success had been based upon a tradition of consultation and consensus, on personal networking and ad hoc arrangements. This has sometimes been called "the ASEAN Way". The habit of consultation, the spirit of give and take, and the ability to evolve consensus out of differences are valuable traditions which we should keep. However, the time has come for ASEAN to strengthen its institutions and to be more rule-based. In this respect there is much that ASEAN can learn from the European Union. Western Europe and Southeast Asia are of course very different. The experience of integration in the European Union therefore cannot be replicated in ASEAN without modification to suit our special circumstances.

In Hanoi, the ASEAN leaders agreed to strengthen the regional surveillance process which the finance ministers had adopted in Manila in 1997. They also agreed to examine the feasibility of an ASEAN currency and an exchange-rate mechanism. This is another area in which ASEAN can learn many lessons from the experience of the European Union.

Cambodia

Sixth, on the admission of Cambodia, there was a difference of opinion within the family. Vietnam, Indonesia and Malaysia were in favour of admitting Cambodia into ASEAN in Hanoi. Singapore, Thailand and the Philippines were in favour of delaying Cambodia's admission until the coalition government had implemented all the elements of their agreement, especially the creation of a Senate. As Prime Minister Goh said, there was a marriage in Cambodia but the couple has not yet solemnised it. The Hanoi compromise was to reaffirm the decision taken at the first informal summit held in Jakarta in December 1996 to admit Cambodia. The actual date of the admission will be decided when the marriage in Cambodia has been solemnised.

Preparing for the 21st Century

In addition to overcoming the present economic crisis and maintaining unity in diversity, ASEAN must also prepare itself for the challenges of the new century. The world is going through a paradigm shift. Globalisation is transforming the world. The world economy will be based increasingly on knowledge. In this borderless world ASEAN will have to re-engineer itself in order to stay in the race. ASEAN will have to rethink its economic strategy from one based on cheap labour to one based on skilled labour. In future, ASEAN may have to worry as much about the quality of growth as about the rate of growth. In the new world, the role of the state will diminish and the role of the market and of civil society will expand. ASEAN's officials should therefore be more open to ideas and inputs from non-state sectors.

Conclusion

ASEAN was on trial in Hanoi. I believe that ASEAN's leaders will rise to the occasion for three reasons. They knew that they had to restore the confidence of investors in the region. They were aware that they live in a region of giants, such as China and Japan. Only by uniting their strength will they be able to play in the same league as China and Japan. Finally, they were aware that, economically, ASEAN is competing with other dynamic regional economies such as the European Union, NAFTA and Mercosur, the South American common market. I am therefore cautiously optimistic that ASEAN will again confound its critics and emerge victorious from its third crisis.

(Article for Institut Français des Relations Internationales (IFRI) Journal – Politique Étrangère, Spring 1999.)

Beyond the Clouds

Introduction

July 1997 will be engraved in the collective memory of East Asians as the month in which the much-feared domino theory toppled the economies of East Asia. In July 1997, the Thai baht was brought down by the international market. The falling Thai domino knocked down the Indonesian, Malaysian and South Korean dominoes. As a result, most of the economies of East Asia, except China and Taiwan, experienced various degrees of contraction. Western critics of East Asia had a field day. Sceptics of the East Asian economic miracle rejoiced at the sight of the fallen dominoes. Other Western critics wrote seemingly learned essays explaining that the crisis was due to the lack of democracy or the bankruptcy of Asian values. I wonder what they would say now that the economies of East Asia are roaring back.

Opening Up

First, the crisis has had the beneficial effect of persuading a number of East Asian economies, such as Indonesia, Thailand, the Philippines, South Korea and Japan, to accelerate the opening of their economies, including sectors which had previously been closed to foreign investment. For example, the car industry in Japan has been transformed. Icons such as Nissan and Mazda are now partially owned by the French and the Americans, respectively. In South Korea, Thailand, the Philippines, Indonesia and Singapore, the banking industry has been liberalised and is open to foreign investment and acquisition. As a result, in the crisis years of 1997 and 1998, Thailand and South Korea received more FDI than in the pre-crisis period. The first fruit of the crisis is therefore the accelerated opening of the economies of East Asia.

Confronting KKN

Second, the crisis has had the beneficial effect of alerting East Asians to the importance of good corporate governance. The Indonesian students' campaign against the three evils of corruption, collusion and nepotism (or KKN) has been taken up by the rest of the region. Asians now realise that in order to run a modern and competitive economy, KKN must be replaced by transparency and accountability. Asian companies and banks are now more willing than before to disclose relevant information to their shareholders and the market.

There is also a regional consensus on the need to conform to international best practice in accounting, auditing and banking. The recommendations of the Bank of International Settlements have acquired a new salience. The international rating agencies have been empowered. The second fruit of the crisis has been the movement in East Asia towards discarding old ways of doing business and embracing the concept of good corporate governance. The victory of this movement is, however, not assured. Too rapid a recovery may defeat the movement.

Uniting East Asia

Third, the crisis has had the beneficial effect of bringing home to East Asians the desirability of uniting the region and building new institutions to serve the region. During the crisis, the region looked helpless when, in fact, it is very rich. Together, Japan, China, Taiwan, Hong Kong and Singapore have US$600 billion worth of foreign exchange reserves, 38 per cent of the world's total. Because the region is not united and because we lack common institutions, we were unable to help each other effectively. This realisation has inspired a number of new ideas and activities.

Japan has proposed the establishment of an Asian Monetary Fund. When Japan first floated the idea, it was shot down by the United States and the IMF. Japan has, however, revived the idea, but it needs to flesh out its proposal. We need answers to the following questions:

- Who will provide the sum of $100 billion to the fund?
- How will it be managed?
- Will it be linked to the IMF?
- Will loans from the fund have the same or different conditionalities as those from the IMF?

Though the proposal raises many questions, it is also one that deserves to be carefully considered.

Japan has also proposed the internationalisation of the Japanese yen, making it, along with the US dollar and the euro, the third international currency of the world. Some Japanese have suggested that if each of the countries of the region should decide to manage its currency against a trade-weighted basket of currencies, the region should study the feasibility of adopting a regional basket. The head of the Hong Kong Monetary Authority, Joseph Yam, has proposed the idea of an Asian monetary union.

Some of these ideas, such as the regional basket of trade-weighted currencies, may not be feasible. Other ideas, such as an Asian monetary union, may take as much as two generations to accomplish. What is interesting is that, for the first time, some of the best minds of the region are thinking about how to unite East Asia and how to build new institutions to serve the region's needs. In March 1999, China initiated the first meeting of the finance ministers and central bank deputies of ASEAN, China, Japan and South Korea (ASEAN + 3) in Hanoi. In April 1999, the finance ministers of ASEAN + 3 met in Manila. Japan has proposed that senior officials of that group should meet to prepare for the next summit and to follow up on decisions taken at each summit. South Korea had proposed the creation of the East Asia Vision Group to formulate a framework for cooperation. The third fruit of the crisis is therefore the impetus it has given to the creation of an East Asian Community.

Too Quick a Recovery?

The currency and economic crisis has brought much pain and destruction to East Asia. However, every dark cloud has a silver lining. The crisis has forced some of the relatively closed economies of the region to open up. It has pushed East Asia away from corruption, collusion and nepotism towards good corporate governance. It has given new momentum to the evolution of an East Asian Community. If East Asians could build upon these developments, the region would emerge from the crisis more competitive and more united than before. But success is not assured. The danger is that the recovery is taking place so quickly that the political will to push through with painful reform and restructuring will be defeated by the power of vested interests.

(*Article published in* Worldlink — *Magazine of the World Economic Forum, September/October 1999.*)

Asia's Stake in the Euro

A giant will be born on 1 January 1999, yet not many Asians are aware of it. In a history-making pooling of sovereignty, 11 independent nations of the European Union will voluntarily give up their national currencies in favour of a common currency, the euro. Euroland — as the grouping of Germany, France, Italy, and eight other countries has come to be known — will have more than a single monetary policy. It will also have a combined population of 290 million people, a combined GDP 50 per cent larger than that of Japan, and a 20 per cent share of world trade.

With most Asian leaders focused on their current economic problems, few have yet thought deeply about the euro. They should do so, because the new currency has great significance for countries so connected to the global economy. First, and most fundamentally, a strong euro could, over time, surpass the Japanese yen and rival the US dollar for international influence. Current indications are that the euro will indeed be strong — and will bring some much-needed balance to the way the world uses its money. At present, although the US constitutes only 25 per cent of the world economy, the US dollar is used in 50 per cent of world trade, and two-thirds of the world's foreign exchange reserves are kept in the American currency. Given Euroland's economic clout, this reliance on the US dollar is likely to change.

Asian governments should welcome the emergence of a strong euro. After all, over-reliance by some Asian countries on the US dollar was one of the causes leading to the East Asian monetary and economic crisis. The Thai baht, for example, was aligned to the US dollar and appreciated along with it. As a result, Thailand lost export competitiveness. It is better for Asian governments to manage their currencies against a trade-weighted basket of currencies, including the US dollar, the yen, the euro and other hard currencies.

There are already signs that some Asian countries are moving toward greater recognition of the euro. That is good for the world's financial stability. Asian governments hold 38 per cent of the world's total foreign exchange reserves, with the bulk of them currently in US-dollar assets. China, however, has already announced that it intends to switch some of its 140 billion in reserves from the US dollar to the euro. Fred Bergsten of the Institute of International Economics in Washington, D.C. has estimated that, over the next five to ten years, there could be a transfer of between US$500 billion and US$1 trillion from the US dollar to the euro. Much of the adjustment will take place in Asia. Robert Mundell of Columbia University has predicted that by 2006 the US dollar and the euro will be on par, each accounting for 40 per cent of the world's reserves.

The huge new capital market that the euro is creating is of great significance for Asians. Asian governments and companies with good credit ratings will be able to raise funds there. The combined European bond markets are already larger than the US market. Unified by the euro, the new market offers opportunity for Asian borrowers and investors alike.

Asians also have a stake in the ongoing streamlining of European business. The euro is making costs totally transparent and fueling a wave of mergers, acquisitions and corporate refocusing. European companies are selling off their non-core businesses — a process that is sure to create investment opportunities for Asian companies. At the same time, a bigger, more vibrant home market is enabling global-minded European companies such as ABN-AMRO, Siemens and Nestlé to expand more confidently in Asia.

But the euro's significance goes well beyond business and finance. Europe aspires to a global role commensurate with its economic power. This is why the European Union has embarked upon its next great adventure, and has begun to forge a common foreign and security policy. This will probably take another generation to accomplish, but sometime in the next century, Churchill's vision of a United States of Europe could become a reality. For Asians, such a development might be a blessing, because it would mean we would no longer be living in a unipolar world.

What can East Asia learn from European unification? A great deal. What the region lacks is not money. The foreign exchange reserves of Japan, China, Hong Kong, Singapore and Taiwan amount to $600 billion. What Asia lacks is unity, a common vision and common institutions. I think the time has come for East Asians to emulate Western Europe and to embark upon the historic journey of building a new, united and prosperous East Asia. True, the first step in that journey — historic reconciliation between Japan and China, and Japan and Korea — has not yet taken place. And as the lack of a breakthrough in President Jiang's recent visit to Japan shows, the process will not be an easy one. But the current economic crisis is an opportunity for East Asian leaders to boost financial and monetary cooperation on several fronts, including a review of Japan's proposal for an Asian Monetary Fund. The Europeans are proving that it is possible to build a superpower on the ruins of old enmities. Asia would be foolish to ignore their example.

(*Article in Newsweek, 21 December 1998.*)

The Euro
Separating Fact from Fiction

Introduction

Since its birth on 1 January 1999, the new European currency, the euro, has steadily depreciated against the US dollar. This has given rise to a steady stream of writing, in the English language press of the world, trashing the euro. I wish to answer some of the questions which have been raised by those writers.

Question

Is it true that the "euro dream" is just a lot of hype?

Answer

It is not true. Monetary union was the final step in the European Union's (EU) steady march towards economic integration. This journey began in 1951 with the relatively modest European Coal and Steel Community. This led to the creation of the European Economic Community in 1958 in the Treaty of Rome. Eight years later, in 1966, the customs union binding the original six member states was completed. In 1973, Denmark, Ireland and the UK joined the EEC. In 1980, Greece joined. In 1986, Portugal and Spain were admitted.

On 1 July 1990, capital movements in the EU member states were fully liberalised. On 1 January 1993, a single market abolishing all internal barriers to trade in goods and services was achieved. The creation of the single market inspired the

European leaders to embrace the goal of monetary union as contained in the Maastricht Treaty of 1993. On 1 January 1994, the European Monetary Institute was established in Frankfurt. The goal of European monetary union was therefore not hype. It was the culmination of Western Europe's vision of creating one integrated and powerful economy. The objective of European integration is, in the final analysis, not about economics. It is about peace. It is about the fulfilment of the post-Second World War European dream of reconciliation and peace.

Question

Is it true that neither the euro's foundation nor the economic fundamentals were sound in the first place?

Answer

It is not true. In order to qualify to be a member of the Eurozone, a country must comply with the convergence criteria of the Maastricht Treaty. What were those criteria? There were five: (i) low inflation; (ii) low long-term interest rates; (iii) stable exchange rates; (iv) government budget deficit of less than 3 per cent of GDP; and (v) gross public debt of less than 60 per cent of GDP. In the run-up to the launch of the euro, the eleven member-states of the Eurozone accepted extraordinary macroeconomic and fiscal discipline. It is therefore factually wrong to say that the euro is not based upon a strong foundation or strong economic fundamentals.

Question

Is it true that the euro has depreciated against the US dollar by about 12 per cent since its launch?

Answer

It is true. On 4 January 1999, the euro hit a high of 1.19 against the US dollar. It has since hit a low of 1.05. This represents a depreciation of about 12 per cent. In trade-weighted terms, however, the euro has depreciated by about 4 per cent compared with the values of its component currencies at the beginning of 1998. In other words, the euro's depreciation against the dollar is partly a reflection of the dollar's strength.

Question

Why has the euro depreciated against the US dollar?

Answer

The main reason for the fall of the euro compared with the US dollar is a shift in the relative growth prospects of Europe and America. In late 1998, most private forecasters expected the Eurozone to grow by 2.6 per cent and the US by 1.9 per cent in 1999. Today, the polls expect that the Eurozone will grow by only 2.1 per cent whereas the US is expected to grow by 3.8 per cent in 1999. Europe's anchor economy, Germany, has done particularly badly and is projected to grow by only 1.4 per cent this year. The US and European economic cycles are not moving in sync. When the US economy slows down and the Eurozone picks up, so will the euro.

Question

Is it true that one reason for the fall in the value of the euro is that no single individual or institution seems to be in charge of the currency?

Answer

It is not true. The European Central Bank (ECB) sets monetary policy for all EU countries within the Eurozone. The ECB works with the national central banks within what is called the European System of Central Banks (ESCB). The ESCB is modelled after the German federalist system and is analogous to the US Federal Reserve System. Decisions are taken by the Governing Council of the ECB. National central banks participate actively in the preparation and implementation of those decisions. The

Governing Council of the ECB consists of the President of the ECB, the heads of the national central banks of the eleven EU countries in the Eurozone and five other full-time members of the executive council.

Question

Who is the European equivalent of Mr Alan Greenspan?

Answer

He is Mr Wim Duisenburg, the President of the ECB.

Question

Is there an institution which is in charge of the euro?

Answer

Yes, it is the Governing Council of the ECB. The problem is that the ECB is not perceived to be completely in control of the euro by the markets. In life, perception is almost as important as reality.

Question

Should the European Union abandon its "Stability and Growth Pact"?

Answer

The answer is no. The Stability and Growth Pact is not a contributory cause to the weakening of the euro.

Question

What are the objectives of the Stability and Growth Pact?

Answer

First, it seeks to coordinate the fiscal policies of the member-states of the Eurozone. This is essential since the Eurozone does not have a federal government and a federal budget. The pact creates an informal forum for close mutual surveillance and coordination.

Second, the pact seeks to prevent well-run economies from having to pay high-risk premiums by punishing those economies which run excessive deficits with penalties.

Third, the pact allows member economies to create a fiscal buffer during good times which can then be drawn on if an asymmetric shock were to occur.

In summary, the Stability and Growth Pact should be maintained and not abandoned because it ensures that the Eurozone will have the features of an optimal monetary zone, with synchronized business cycles, an appropriate policy mix and the ability to absorb asymmetric shocks.

Question

Does the fall in the value of the euro mean that it is a failure?

Answer

No, it does not. On the contrary, most Europeans would regard the launch of the euro as a success rather than a failure. Why?

First, the euro has brought about the speedy and trouble-free integration of the financial markets of Europe.

Second, European stock markets are close to record high.

Third, the euro has created a European bond market which is bigger than that of the US. For example, in the first four months of 1999, European industrial companies issued bonds equivalent to 32.7 billion euros compared with 7.4 billion euros in the same period in 1998.

Fourth, Europe's consumers are going to benefit as companies reduce their prices to the lower prices they use in their most competitive markets.

Fifth, European companies must compete, merge, acquire, to survive in the new integrated European market. Mergers and acquisitions are booming at five times the peak of the previous level.

Question

Does the fall in the value of the euro also reflect internal economic weaknesses in the Eurozone?

Answer

Yes, it does. Eurozone's economies face some serious structural problems. The Eurozone needs to attack its high taxes, over-generous welfare benefits, labour market rigidities and bureaucratic red tape. Eurozone needs to focus on how to facilitate the restructuring of European business so that it will become more competitive.

Question

Should the European Central Bank have intervened to prop up the value of the euro?

Answer

Some writers have criticised the ECB for its policy of "benign neglect". The critics would have liked the ECB to intervene in the foreign exchange markets in order to prevent the slide in the value of the euro. I think the criticism is misconceived. We live in a world in which the daily foreign exchange transactions amount to US$1.6 trillion. In such a world, intervention in foreign exchange markets seldom works unless it is supported by economic fundamentals. The *raison d'être* of the ECB is to fight inflation and maintain price stability. Inflation is not a problem as the current inflation rate of the Eurozone is only 1 per cent. Raising interest rates would be the wrong thing to do in view of the current weak growth in the Eurozone. In fact, a cheaper euro may be a good thing as it could boost exports and growth.

Question

Does the fall in the value of the euro mean that it is not an important currency and will not be a rival of the US dollar?

Answer

The euro is an important currency. This is because the Eurozone represents an economy almost as large as the US economy. When the remaining four EU countries join the Eurozone, it will be larger than the US economy. The Eurozone enjoys larger trade flows and has more monetary reserves than the US. Unlike the US, which has a net foreign debt of US$2 trillion, the Eurozone is a net creditor. Whether the euro will become an important reserve currency rivalling the US dollar only time will tell. If the euro becomes a strong and stable currency, other countries will want to have part of their reserves in euro. If the euro becomes a weak and unstable currency other countries will obviously not want to do so. It is as simple as that. It is therefore premature at this stage to make any predictions. What can be safely said is that the creation of the euro is historically unprecedented and that it has the potential to become the world's second most important currency.

(*Article written for* The Sunday Times, Sunday Review. *Published on 20 June 1999 with the title "Early Days Yet for Euro".*)

Launch of the Asia-Europe Foundation (ASEF) at 1 Nassim Hill, Singapore (February 1997)

Logging on the newly launched ASEF website (August 1997)

Leading the Management Team of ASEF.
(*From left to right*) Ulrich Niemann, Terence Tan, Pierre Barroux, Tommy Koh, Peggy Kek, Cai Rongsheng and Duncan Jackman.

Hosting a delegation of Finland's Ambassadors to Asia (December 1998)

Meeting with Emiliano Fossati of the European Commission (December 1997)

Dinner on the occasion of the Colloquium on Human Rights and Human Responsibilities in Hamburg, Germany (November 1998)

First ASEF Meeting of Editors in Luxembourg (October 1997)

Inaugural Asia-Europe Lecture (January 1998)

With Sotirios Mousouris (ASEF Greek Governor) and Patrick van Haute (Former ASEF Belgian Governor) on the occasion of the 3rd ASEF Board Meeting in Bangkok (February 1998)

Exchanging books with HE MR Sukhumbhand Paribatra, Thai Deputy Minister of Foreign Affairs (February 1998)

Launch of the First ASEF Summer School (July 1998)

Introducing Ambassador Luz del Mundo, ASEF Governor for the Philippines, to HE Mr Jozias J van Aartsen, Foreign Minister of the Netherlands (October 1998)

Chairing the Second ASEF Colloquium for Journalists in Jakarta, Indonesia (May 1999)

Introducing Pierre Barroux to HE Mr Juwono Sudarsono, Indonesian Cabinet Minister (May 1999)

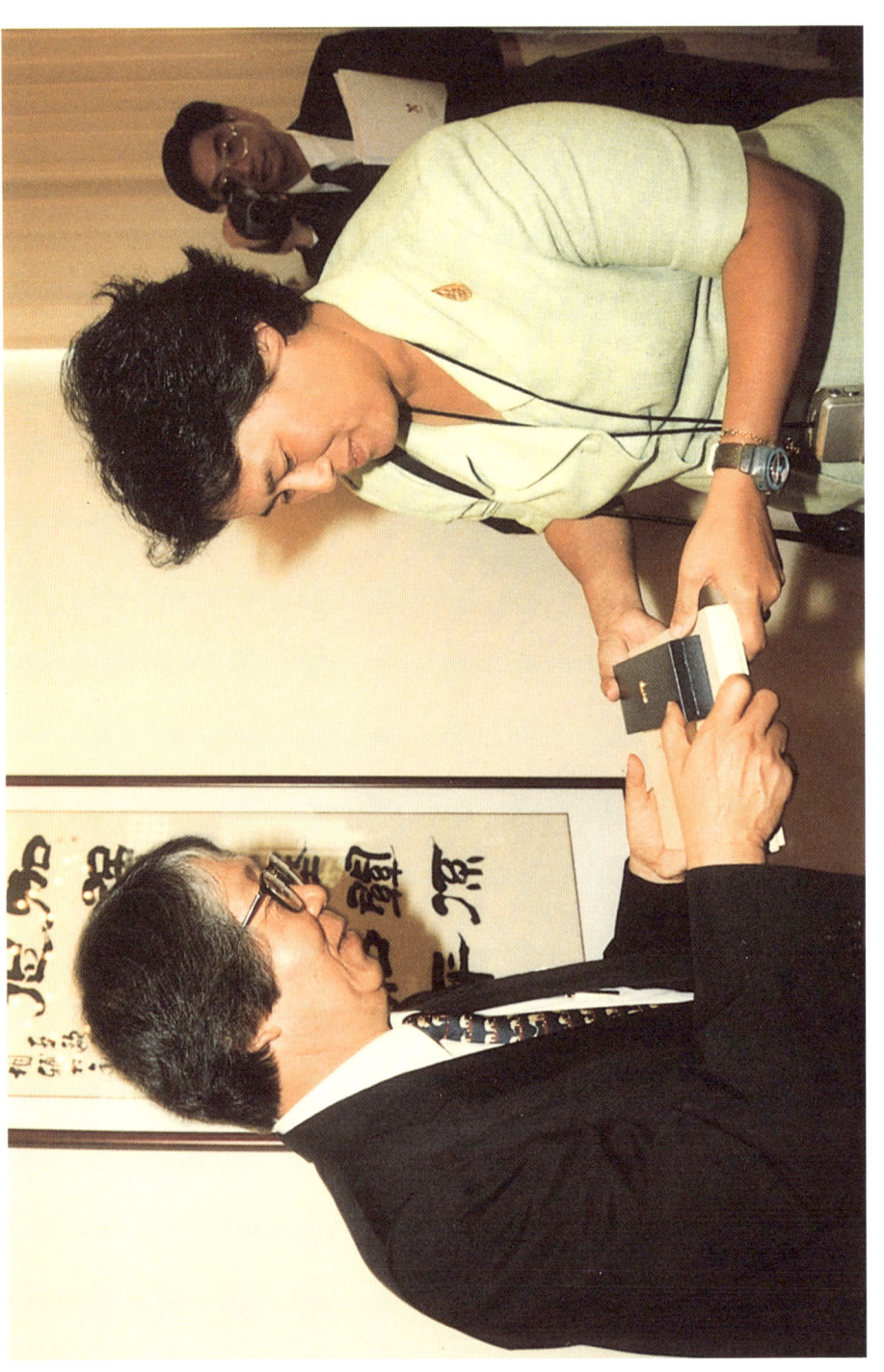

Hosting Thai Princess HRH Maha Chakri Sirindhorn at ASEF (February 1999)

Hosting the former President of the Philippines, His Excellency Fidel Ramos at ASEF (September 1998)

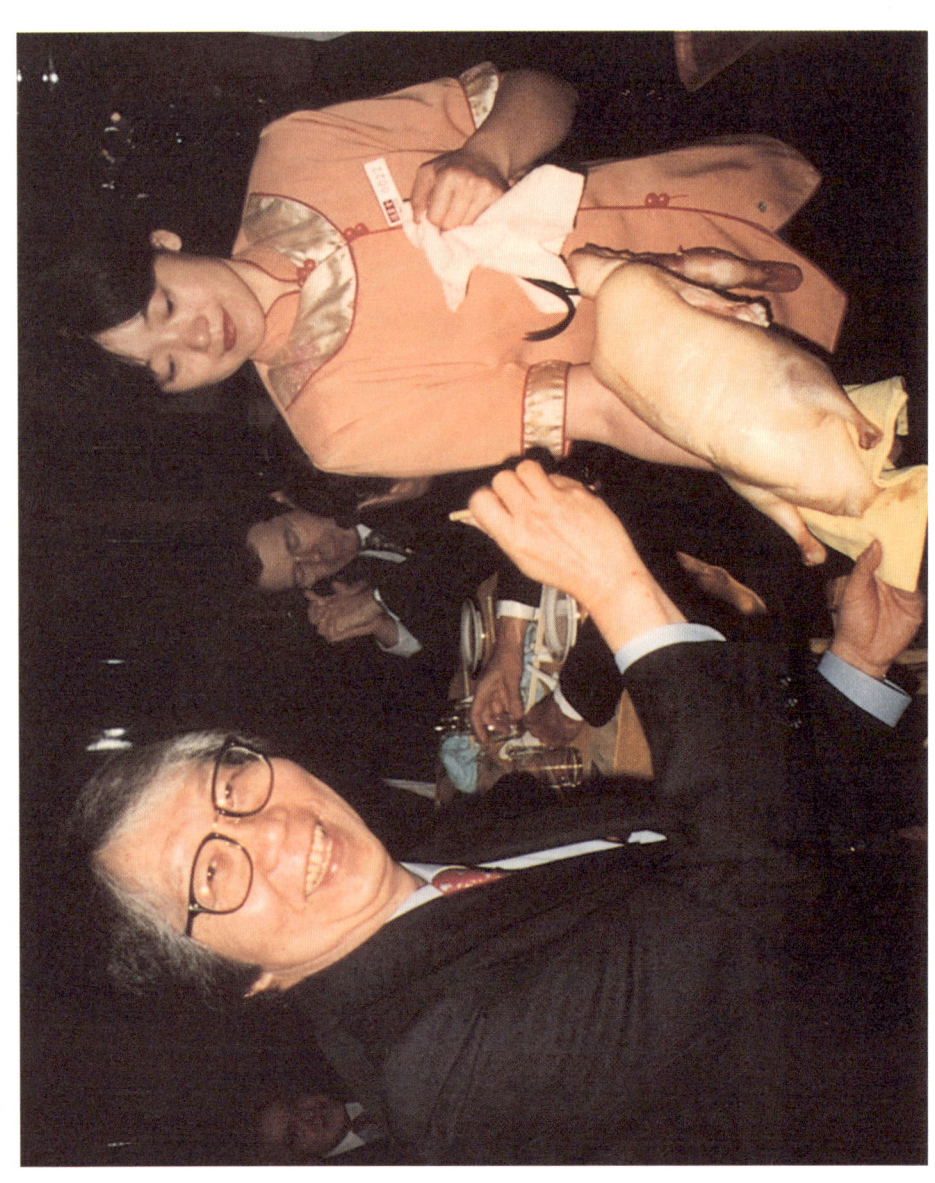

Dinner on the occasion of the Second ASEM Informal Human Rights Seminar in Beijing (May 1999)

With participants of Europe Asia Forum 2000 in Singapore (April 2000)

With Professor Christopher Tan at the Education Conference in Luxembourg (May 2000)

Interviewing HRH Prince Henri, Crown Prince of Luxembourg, for a Channel News Asia TV documentary on Asia-Europe relations (January 2000)

Europe Asia Forum 2000, Singapore (April 2000)

A NEW ASIA AND A NEW EUROPE

What is their future likely to be? In answering the question, these essays explore how the two regions are responding to common global forces. Interestingly, not all those forces are new.

Europe and East Asia
Need to Get Acquainted

There is a huge knowledge gap between Asians and Europeans. This is partly because America's image looms very large in the contemporary world.

Since the breakup of the Soviet Union, the United States has become the world's only superpower, with the economic muscle to match its military might. The French foreign minister, Hubert Vedrine, has even described the United States as a hyperpower.

The US economy accounts for 25 per cent of the world economy. But that is significantly less than the share of the European Union (EU), 29 per cent. It is the EU, not the US, that has the world's largest economy.

In the 1997–1998 East Asian monetary and economic crisis, many Asians criticised Europe for doing too little to help. Most believed that the US helped East Asia more than Europe did. Yet the reality is that the EU contributed more than America to the IMF's rescue packages for Thailand, Indonesia and South Korea. The EU's contribution was 18.8 per cent, and America's was 15.6 per cent. Europe has not received the credit it deserves because the facts are not well known and the Europeans are not as good in marketing themselves as the Americans.

Who is East Asia's largest creditor? The general impression in Asia is that it must be either Japan or the US. Yet banks from the EU countries have loaned more money to East Asia than their Japanese or American counterparts. Total loans of EU banks to East Asia amounted to $106 billion. The figure for

Japanese banks is $68 billion, while for the US banks it is only $18 billion.

If East Asians are generally not aware that the EU economy is larger than the US economy, most Europeans also have no idea about the size of the East Asian economy, which includes China, Japan, South Korea, Brunei, Indonesia, Malaysia, the Philippines, Singapore, Thailand and Vietnam. As a result, many Europeans still think of East Asia as a region of backward countries and wrongly perceive trade as a threat rather than as an opportunity.

One measure of economic stability and potential spending power is surplus foreign exchange reserves. East Asia's foreign exchange reserves amount to $693.7 billion, the EU's to $384.8 billion, and the US' to $60.5 billion.

In 1996, the year before the economic crisis, the ten economies of East Asia accounted for 25 per cent of world GDP, the same as the US. In the same year, trade between the EU and the US was worth $295.42 billion while that between the EU and East Asia was $308.02 billion.

As a result of the crisis, the EU's trade with East Asia from 1997 to 1999 was less than with America. But many East Asian economies are growing strongly again, and once the region has fully recovered, it will again be Europe's largest trading partner.

Europe's contact with East Asia goes back further than any other region of the world. It could be traced to Marco Polo's historic journey to China 800 years ago. Five hundred years ago, the great Portuguese explorers, Vasco da Gama and Magellan were the first Europeans to reach the shores of India, China, Japan and the Philippines.

In the past 500 years, East Asia has been greatly influenced by Western Europe in all spheres of life. The Europeans brought Christianity to East Asia. The democratic ideals and values of Plato, the Magna Carta and Rousseau have influenced the political ideals of Asian thinkers. European scientists such as Newton and Einstein; writers such as Dante, Shakespeare and Goethe; and musicians such as Bach, Beethoven, Chopin and

Mozart, are much admired by Asians. Although East Asia is catching up with Western Europe economically, its people wish to continue to learn from Europe.

East Asia has also influenced Western Europe in many ways. The technologies for making gunpowder and porcelain were imported from East Asia. The writings of Confucius and Sun Tze are well known to European intellectuals. Buddhism, Taoism and Shintoism have been studied by European scholars for centuries. Some great European artists, such as Matisse and Picasso, were influenced by East Asian art.

There is much that each region can learn from the other. They have some important things in common. East Asia and the EU share a common vision of the future. They want to build a peaceful and prosperous multipolar world. They accept globalisation but also want to live in a world of cultural diversity.

East Asia and Europe want economic growth, but they also value social equity, a healthy environment and a rich cultural life. They want to embrace the new economy but they also aim to strike a balance between chaos and order.

We need to be reminded that while the US is important to Asia and the world, the EU, too, is important. It will become more important as the Union expands and integrates further.

(*Article published in the International Herald Tribune, 14 April 2000.*)

East Asia in the 21st Century

Introduction

As I am neither a futurologist nor a scenario-planner, I will not attempt to forecast the future or to paint scenarios of the future. I will, instead, describe three visions of what East Asia could be in the 21st century. A word about East Asia before I proceed. By East Asia, I mean the countries of Northeast Asia, namely, China (including Hong Kong and Taiwan), Japan and Korea, and the countries of Southeast Asia. A sense of community is emerging among the countries of this sub-region of Asia. This sense of community is being driven by intra-regional trade and investment, by common challenges such as the monetary and economic crisis of the past three years, and by the necessity to consult before joining the European Union and the United States in such forums as the Asia–Europe Meeting (ASEM) and the Asia–Pacific Economic Cooperation (APEC), respectively.

Vision No. 1: A World-Class Economy

My first vision is that East Asia could have a world-class economy in the 21st century. In the past 30 years, East Asia has made very impressive economic progress. In 1965, it accounted for only 9 per cent of the world economy. By 1975, its share had gone up to 15 per cent. By 1995, East Asia had caught up with the United States, each accounting for 25 per cent of the world economy. The European Union's share was slightly higher at 29 per cent. According to some analysts, by the first half of the 21st century, East Asia's economy will be larger than those of the United States and the European Union combined.

Size is, however, not enough. What must East Asia do in order to build a world-class economy? It must jettison the KKN way of doing business. The acronym KKN refers, in Bahasa Indonesia, to corruption, collusion and nepotism. The old way of doing business in some of the economies of East Asia depends upon political connections, kickbacks and special privileges. The old way is incompatible with a world-class economy and should be abandoned. East Asia should embrace the concept of good corporate governance, which emphasises the virtues of transparency and accountability. This is, of course, easier said than done. The KKN culture is deeply embedded in many of the countries of East Asia. During the past three years, because of the monetary and economic crisis, attempts have been made in countries such as Korea and Thailand to abandon the old way in favour of good corporate governance. The struggle between the reformists and the vested interests continues. Victory for the reformists is by no means assured.

There is another challenge. The world economy is being transformed. In the 21st century, it will be driven by knowledge, innovation, creativity and new technologies such as information technology. East Asia will not be able to compete with the West unless it embraces the new technologies, upgrades its schools, polytechnics and universities to world-class standards, boosts productivity and fosters the growth of innovation and creativity. The last will be the most difficult to accomplish. Changing mindsets is a formidable task. East Asia will have to make a paradigm shift from its old culture which emphasises hierarchy and consensus to a new culture which fosters critical thinking and innovation. My vision of East Asia with a world-class economy can only come true if East Asia succeeds in overcoming those two challenges.

Vision No. 2: An East Asian Cultural Renaissance

My second vision is that East Asia could enjoy a cultural renaissance in the 21st century. I see many evidence of such a movement taking place. Culture and the arts have become increasingly important to the national agendas of the countries of East Asia and to the personal aspirations of a new generation of East Asians. New artistic infrastructure, such as museums, theatres, symphony halls and opera houses, is being built. More and better cultural festivals are being staged. Audiences are expanding. Sponsorship of the arts by Asian business is growing.

A new generation of East Asian artists has emerged and is making a major impact on the region and the world. Filmmakers such as Zhang Yimou and Chen Kaige of China, Lee Ang of Taiwan and John Woo of Hong Kong are admired throughout the world. Actors and actresses such as Jackie Chan, Chow Yuen Fatt, Jet Li, Gong Li, Joan Chen and Michelle Yeoh have won international stardom. In the world of high fashion, the three Japanese icons, Hanae Mori, Kenzo and Issey Miyake, have put Asia on the map. There are other rising stars in the worlds of music, dance, theatre, visual art and literature.

Another interesting phenomenon is that East Asians are developing a new interest in each other's culture. This is true of the audience as well as the artists. As a result, interesting cross-fertilisation is taking place between the arts of different Asian countries. A successful example is the pan-Asian production of "Lear", directed by Ong Keng Sen of Singapore, written by a Japanese playwright, and involving actors, singers, dancers and musicians from China, Japan, Indonesia, Malaysia, Singapore and Thailand.

My hope is that in the 21st century East Asia will not only be an economic power, it will also be a cultural power. In that future, East Asia will not be a mere consumer of Western cultural products. East Asia could also be a producer of world-class films, TV programmes, music, dance, drama, painting, sculpture, photography, books, magazines, fashion and food, which would be exported to the rest of the world.

Vision No. 3: Asian Models of Good Government

My third vision is that East Asia could evolve its own models of democracy and good government. It is important to point out that the two concepts are not the same. A good government has to be a democratic government. However, not all democratic governments are good governments. My starting point is that all human beings aspire to live under a good government. What is my concept of a good government?

First, a good government should be a democratic government in the sense that it is a government chosen by the people and accountable to the people. There is, however, no universal model of democracy. For example, the British, American, French and German models of democracy are not identical and contain different characteristics. It is therefore entirely legitimate for the various East Asian countries to evolve their own models of democracy which are rooted in their history, culture and context. I do not, however, expect East Asia to evolve a single model of democracy but a variety of them. I do expect that some East Asian democracies will contain uniquely Asian features. I also expect East Asian democratic cultures to be infused with communitarian values.

Second, a good government should provide for the basic human needs of its citizens. What are they? They include employment, housing, health care, education, peace and security and a clean environment. I have included a peaceful and secure environment as a basic human need because we do not want to live in constant fear for our safety. Why a clean environment? Because we want to live in an environment in which we can drink the water; breathe the air; have access to modern sanitation; swim in our rivers, lakes and seas; and live in harmony with nature.

Third, a good government should observe the rule of law and respect the human rights of its citizens. The rule of law is very weak in several of the countries of East Asia. Historically, the rule of man has been stronger than the rule of law in many parts of East Asia. A modern East Asia must uphold the rule of law and not the rule of man. East Asia has to complete its transition from the rule of man to the rule of law. On human rights, I expect continued progress in East Asia. I do not, however, expect East Asia and the West to hold identical views on human rights even in the 21st century. This is because there is a fundamental cultural difference between the individual-centred civilisation of the West and the group-centred civilisation of the East. The picture is, however, not static. The world is changing. East Asia is changing. A new generation of East Asians is coming of age. The new generation will be more individualistic and more assertive of its rights. Thus, I expect the individual in East Asia to be increasingly empowered in the 21st century. I expect civil society to grow. I expect a new equilibrium to emerge between the individual, his family and society.

In the next century, East Asia will have successful models of Asian democracy and good government. I hope East Asia will represent some transcendental ideals of government which will be admired by the world. If my vision is realised, East Asia will no longer be on the defensive in its dialogue with the West. Instead, East Asia will bring to the dialogue its own positive ideas of how to govern society and how to calibrate the relationship between the individual and the state.

Conclusion

We stand on the threshold of an important milestone, the end of the 20th century and the beginning of the 21st century. The first half of this century was not a good period for East Asia. Things began to improve in the third quarter. It was, however, only the fourth quarter of the 20th century that saw East Asia taking off and catching up with the West. The prospects are bright for East Asia in the 21st century. I believe that it is possible for East Asia to build a world-class economy, enjoy a cultural renaissance and evolve East Asian models of democracy and good government. With great effort and good luck, it is possible to build a New Asia, one which is modern, prosperous, cultured and humane.

(*Adapted from speech given at the Inaugural Raffles Lecture in Singapore on 1 October 1999. This speech was published in the Harvard Asia Pacific Review, Winter 2000 issue.*)

Singapore
A New Venice of the 21st Century

Introduction

Venice is one of the legendary cities of the world. Its beauty and physical setting make it unique. For almost 800 years, from AD 1000 to 1797, the Venetians were a separate people. It was therefore one of the world's longest surviving city-states. The great historian of Venice, Frederic C Lane, wrote that "among the many cities men have made, Venice stands out as a symbol of beauty, of wise government, and of communally controlled capitalism... a city renowned for its skills in handicraft, finance and government."[a]

In 1802, William Wordsworth wrote the following poem, "On the Extinction of the Venetian Republic":

> Once did she hold the gorgeous East in fee;
> And was the safeguard of the West: the worth
> Of Venice did not fall below her birth,
> Venice, the eldest child of Liberty.
> She was a maiden city, bright and free;
> No guile seduced, no force could violate;
> And, when she took unto herself a Mate,
> She must expouse the everlasting Sea.
> And what if she had seen those glories fade,
> Those titles vanish, and that strength decay;

---

[a] Lane, Frederic C, *Venice, A Maritime Republic*. Baltimore, Maryland and London: The Johns Hopkins University Press, 1973:1.

Yet shall some tribute of regret be paid
When her long life has reached its final day:
Men are we, and must grieve when even the Shade
Of that which once was great is pass'd away.

My Fascination with Venice

It is natural for a Singaporean, a citizen of the only city-state in the contemporary world, to be fascinated with Venice. I realised my childhood dream of visiting Venice only in June 1997. I marvelled at the genius of the ancient Venetians in overcoming the odds and building such a beautiful city on the sea. I reflected on the fact that Singapore is a city built by the sea, and, like Venice, lives on the sea. As I walked along the cobbled streets and crossed the many bridges of Venice, I remembered that this was the home of Marco Polo, the first European explorer to visit China in 1271 and whose book, *Description of the World*, published in 1295, astonished the Western world. Standing in the Piazza di San Marco (Saint Mark's Square), I wondered what magical combination of good policies, institutions and leaders had enabled Venice to achieve and maintain the status of a great power for 200 years from 1281 to 1481.[b] I went in search of the Jewish and Armenian communities which, along with many others, had flourished in cosmopolitan Venice. I attended a service on Sunday in the Armenian Cathedral and visited its Library to look for information on the Armenian community in Singapore.

Lessons Learnt

What lessons did I learn from my visit to and readings on Venice which are relevant to Singapore? First, one ingredient of Venetian success was national unity. The Venetians were united whereas some of their rival cities, for example, Genoa, were

---

[b] McNeill, WH, *Venice: The Hinge of Europe, 1081–1797*. Chicago: The Chicago University Press, 1974.

divided. Second, the Venetians enjoyed good government. The central organs of government formed a pyramid, with the General Assembly at its base and the doge (duke) at its apex. In between were the Great Council, the Forty and the Senate, and the Ducal Council. The doge was elected by a nominating committee of wise men. Frederic Lane observed: "Distrust of individual power made the Venetians depend on committees and councils. Even in their judicial system, sentences were not imposed by an individual judge but by several judges acting together. Each committee or council was checked by some other committee or council so as to assure the rule of law, even at the cost of losing some executive efficiency."[c] Therefore, although the Venetian Republic was not a democracy, the Venetians did enjoy good governance.

Third, Venice prospered because it used its maritime power to enforce freedom of navigation. Freedom of navigation is crucial to maritime trade. Even today, the bulk of world trade is seaborne. However, unlike the past, an increasing share of world trade is airborne. Electronic commerce has become a reality and is expected to grow exponentially. Singapore must therefore support the freedom of navigation at sea, in the air, as well as on the internet.

Fourth, Venice was both a trading and a financial centre. It pioneered a commercial revolution in the 14th century in Europe. Resident agents took the place of travelling merchants. Family partnerships, in which one brother would stay in Venice while the others would live abroad, became common. Non-family partnerships, joint ventures, the system of double-entry book-keeping, the bill of lading, the bill of exchange and marine insurance were evolved to facilitate trade. For centuries, Venice was an important trading centre linking Europe with Turkey, the Arab world and the East. Venice was also a source of capital to finance trade, the crusades and various kings and princes of Europe. Banking developed in Venice in the 12th

---

[c]Lane, *op. cit.*, p. 95.

century. Until the Church prohibited usury, Venetian creditors used to charge 20 per cent interest on well-secured loans. After the prohibition, Venice developed its own standard of what was legitimate gain. It approved as non-usurious the payment of a rate of return determined by market conditions, much as we do today.

Fifth, I was impressed by the reputation for competence and professionalism of Venetian leaders, admirals, diplomats, shipbuilders, glass blowers, and other artisans. The Venetians excelled in war and in peace. The talent and ability of the Venetian leaders and citizens was one of the necessary ingredients of the success of the city-state. This lesson is timeless. It is as relevant to present-day Singapore as it will be to Singapore in the 21st century.

To sum up, the five lessons which I have learnt from ancient Venice, which are relevant to Singapore, are:

1. The importance of national unity;
2. The crucial role of good governance;
3. The fact that the fate of a nation is ultimately dependent upon the quality of its people and its leaders;
4. The value of freedom of navigation on the sea, and by extension, in the air and on the Internet; and
5. The imperative for Singapore to maintain its pre-eminence as an international trading and financial centre.

(Abridged version of speech delivered at the Sixth SGH Lecture, 26 April 1998.)

The Nordic Community
A View from East Asia

Introduction

Geographically, the five Nordic countries, Denmark, Finland, Iceland, Norway and Sweden, are a long way from East Asia. In this essay I wish to give a personal perspective of what comes to my mind when I think of Scandinavia.

Hans Christian Andersen

Children throughout the world love fairy tales. As a child I read many of the fairy tales of the great Danish writer, Hans Christian Andersen. Some of his classics include "The Emperor's New Clothes", "The Ugly Duckling", "The Snow Queen", "The Nightingale" and "The Red Shoes". I remember how thrilled I was to see the little mermaid, one of Andersen's inventions, in Copenhagen. Danny Kaye's performance, in a Hollywood movie, in the role of Andersen has helped to entrench him in the world's pantheon of writers. Hans Christian Andersen is certainly a Nordic icon.

First Encounter with Denmark

In the summer of 1965 I visited Denmark on my way home from Cambridge University. I stayed at a students' hostel in Copenhagen. One day I went to a post office to mail a letter to my parents. Seeing my uncertainty about which queue to join, a

Danish woman with two young children in tow asked if she could help me. After solving my dilemma she waited for me. She asked me where I was from and whether I had any friends in Copenhagen. When she learnt that I had none she invited me to have dinner with her and her family on the following evening. I was overwhelmed by her kindness to a complete stranger. I kept in touch with her and her husband, a professional photographer, for many years until their marriage broke up and they divorced. She remarried and followed her second husband to Germany. Her first husband has retired and lives outside Copenhagen. Ever since that happy experience I have been a Danophile.

Sweden: Paradise on Earth?

In the summer of 1964 I worked as an intern at the United Nations in New York. One of my colleagues, Terence Carlbom, was from Sweden. In the following summer I visited Sweden as Terence's guest. My first impression of Sweden was that it was almost like paradise on earth. The country was prosperous and wealth was being equitably distributed. There were no slums and no beggars. The environment was clean and green. The public transportation was efficient and affordable. The Swedes had a very high quality of life.

I returned to Sweden in December 1997, thirty-two years after my first visit. I had a happy reunion with my old friend Terry Carlbom, together with his wife and their son. I attended the Nobel Prize Award Ceremony and marveled at the fact that some of the most prestigious prizes of the world were being awarded by a country of only 10 million people. I went from Stockholm to Lund, a university town, to participate in an Asian–European meeting on human rights. I will always remember the closing dinner which was held on a night to honour "Santa Lucia", an Italian saint adopted by Sweden. At a certain moment during the dinner the room was darkened. A youth choir entered the darkened room. They were all dressed in white and looked like angels. The young women wore crowns with lighted candles. They proceeded to serenade us and stole our hearts.

The Third Way Is the Nordic Way

I am convinced that the Third Way, the path between capitalism and socialism which is being sought by leaders such as Tony Blair and Gerhard Schroeder, already exists. The Third Way is the Nordic Way. The Nordic countries can help the world to figure out how to develop capitalism with social equity and globalisation with a human face.

Contributions to World Peace and Global Governance

The Nordic countries have made a disproportionate number of contributions to world peace and global governance. The first Secretary-General of the United Nations, Trygve Lie, was from Norway. The second Secretary-General, Dag Hammarskjold, was from Sweden. From 1945 to 1961, a period of 16 years, the UN Secretariat was therefore led by two remarkable Scandinavian statesmen. Hammarskjold was killed in a plane crash while on a peace mission to the Congo in 1961. That same year he was posthumously awarded the Nobel Peace Prize.

Another remarkable contribution to world peace was made by Norway. It helped to broker the peace agreement between Israel and the PLO. It has been reported recently that Norway is seeking to bring peace to the troubled land of Sri Lanka. Recently, the President of Finland, Maarti Ahtisaari, played a key role in negotiating an end to NATO's air war against Serbia over Kosovo.

I wish also to refer to the Nordic countries' extraordinary contributions to disarmament, peace-keeping, the environment, the law of the sea and helping the developing countries. I recall the critical role played by Sweden's Alva Myrdal in negotiating the Nuclear Non-Proliferation Treaty (NPT). The Nordic countries have contributed generously to many of the UN's peace-keeping operations. The first UN Conference on the Environment was held in Stockholm in 1972. Several distinguished Scandinavian lawyers and diplomats, such as Jens Evensen of Norway, Hans Anderson and Gudmundur Eiriksson of Iceland and Timo Lahelma of Finland, made signal contributions to the Third UN Conference on the Law of the Sea. The Nordic countries have always been more than generous in their official development assistance (ODA).

My overall impression is that the Nordic countries rank among the best global citizens of the world. The paradox today is that we have never been more interdependent or more interconnected, and yet the support in the West for international civil society has never been so weak. We need the Nordic countries to help us mobilise public opinion in the West to support global governance and global public goods. Although the Cold War's division of the world between East and West has disappeared, there is a danger that in the 21st century, the world will again be divided. This time, the division will be between those who are able to benefit from globalisation and others who will fall further behind.

Culture and the Arts

Another thought which comes to my mind when I think of the Nordic countries is their contributions to literature, music, art, architecture and good design. I have already referred to Hans Christian Andersen. Other Scandinavian writers who have contributed to world literature include Norway's Henrik Ibsen and Sweden's August Strindberg. Plays by Ibsen, such as "A Doll's House" and "Hedda Gabler", have been translated into many languages and are classics. Strindberg is Sweden's greatest writer and the father of modern Swedish drama and fiction.

Music is another field in which the Nordic countries have made significant contributions. My favourite Scandinavian composer is Jean Sibelius of Finland. His seven symphonies evoke images of the Finnish landscape through intense orchestral harmonies and folk motifs. I also like his patriotic work "Finlandia". In the contemporary world, Finland has produced a rich harvest of opera singers and orchestral conductors. Denmark, on the other hand, has excelled in ballet.

In the field of architecture, Finland has produced three world-class architects: Eero Saarinen, Eliel Saarinen and Alvar Aalto. All the Nordic countries excel in design. Scandinavian furniture, porcelain, glass and silverware are both exquisite and functional. The hi-fi equipment of Bang & Olufsen is both beautiful and technically superior.

I would like to suggest to the Nordic countries the possibility of establishing joint Nordic Cultural Centres in key cities throughout the world. I envisage such centres as playing the same roles as the UK's British Council, France's Alliance Française and Germany's Goethe Institut. The Nordic countries have a rich cultural heritage to share with the rest of the world. In return, the centres can help the peoples of Scandinavia to develop better understanding of and appreciation for the cultures of other regions of the world. In this way, culture can become a bridge connecting the peoples of the Nordic countries with the rest of the world. I am very pleased to be writing this essay on the day of the opening of the Nordic Film Festival in Singapore.

World Class in Business and Industry

The Nordic countries have also excelled in business and industry. It is truly remarkable that Finland and Sweden are two of the leading countries in the world in telecommunications. Finland's Nokia and Sweden's Ericsson are generally regarded as two of the best brand names in the very competitive field of mobile phones. Denmark's shipping line, Maersk, is one of the world's biggest and best shipping and logistics companies. Volvo and Saab are two of the most respected brand names in automobiles. As the world makes a transition to a knowledge-based economy, creativity and innovation will become more important than land, labour and capital. The Nordic countries, with a high standard in education and an environment which supports high technology, especially information technology, are well positioned to seize the opportunities of the new economy.

Conclusion

The world is going through a paradigm shift. It is being transformed by the process of globalisation and the power of the new technologies. In the new world, size is less important than quality. Land, labour and capital are less important in a borderless world than in the old world where national borders are sacrosanct. The new world offers the Nordic countries many new opportunities which they should exploit. At the same time, it is my hope that they will help the world to evolve new institutions of global governance, reduce the disparities within and between countries, and forge a new consensus on international cooperation in the 21st century.

(*Essay written at the invitation of the Danish Minister for Culture, 10 January 2000.*)

THE BRIDGE-BUILDER
The Asia–Europe Foundation

ASEF is an intellectual entrepreneur. In four short years, it has established itself as an interpreter between Asia and Europe. What will that role entail in the future? Read on.

Report Card on the Asia–Europe Foundation

Mr Chairman, distinguished Leaders, on behalf of the Asia–Europe Foundation (ASEF) and, on behalf of my colleague, Mr Pierre Barroux, I wish to thank you for giving me this privilege to submit a report card on ASEF to you for your scrutiny and approval. In the five minutes allocated to me, I wish to make five points.

First, at the inaugural summit in Bangkok in March 1996, the leaders of Asia and Europe decided to embark upon the historic task of building a new bridge connecting a new Asia and a new Europe. This bridge will rest on four strong foundations: politics, business, public sector and civil society. Our leaders decided to establish the Asia–Europe Foundation in order to bring about the engagement of our two civil societies.

Second, ASEF was born in Singapore on 15 February 1997. Although we are only one year old, we have been a precocious baby. We have implemented 15 projects, with a professional staff of only 7 persons and a budget of less than US$2 million. We have been able to do so much with so little because our guiding philosophy has been to be proactive and not reactive, to add value and avoid duplication, to act as a catalyst and facilitator and not as a banker, and to be inclusive by working with good partners and on a cost-sharing basis.

Third, we understand the importance of enhancing people-to-people exchanges, especially among the young between Asia and Europe. We helped Prime Minister Hashimoto implement the very successful Asia–Europe Young Leaders Symposium in Miyazaki. We shall be holding a summer school for outstanding university students in Germany this year. We plan to convene a meeting of young parliamentarians in November in Asia. In September we shall be launching a pilot project in Copenhagen to twin high schools in Asia and Europe by using the Internet. Last month, ASEF and the British Council brought together 60 brilliant young leaders to discuss the theme "Societies in Transition".

Fourth, ASEF has worked hard to build bridges among our universities, think-tanks, scholars, journalists, and other opinion-makers. We convened the first meeting in Luxembourg last October of 43 news editors from television, radio and newspapers. The President of the European Commission Jacques Santer, honoured us by inaugurating the Asia–Europe Lecture series in Singapore. The highly respected former prime minister of Thailand, Anand Panyarachun, delivered the second lecture on the important nexus between good economic management and good governance. Last month, ASEF in partnership with a German Foundation and a Singapore think-tank co-convened the first Europe–Asia Forum which brought together over 60 leading personalities from the two regions for two days of vigorous and collegial dialogue. In May this year, we shall be bringing some of Asia's top economists to speak at a conference in Paris on the causes of the East Asian economic crisis, the lessons learnt and the prospects for recovery. In June, we shall be bringing three leading European experts on a roadshow to explain the European Monetary Union in the financial centres of Tokyo, Hong Kong and Singapore. In November, we shall be celebrating the 50th anniversary of the Universal Declaration of Human Rights by co-organising with the German paper *Die Zeit* a colloquium in Hamburg to brainstorm the relationship between human rights and human responsibilities.

Fifth, Asia and Europe are the homes of some of the world's most vibrant cultures. We have so much to offer each other. There are so many opportunities for our artists to meet, to learn from one another, to inspire and influence one another and to create together. We should do more to showcase the rich diversity of our cultures to an increasingly receptive public. Culture can help to break down the walls of indifference, prejudice and ignorance. Towards this end, ASEF co-convened with France a very successful cultural forum in Paris which brought together five cultural and artistic leaders from each of the ASEM countries. Seven specific projects were endorsed at the concluding session of the forum. Here in London, ASEF is co-sponsoring with the Visiting Arts of the UK a festival of cultural and artistic events.

I shall conclude. I believe in the historic importance of the task which we began in Bangkok. It is to build a strong bridge between Asia and Europe, complementing the bridges spanning the Atlantic and the Pacific. I believe that the 21st century will be a trilateral world. I also believe that the 21st century will be increasingly open, interconnected and multicultural. To prosper we need not only open markets but also open minds and open hearts. It is the modest ambition of ASEF to help create a new generation of Asians and Europeans whose minds and hearts are open to each other.

(*Statement on ASEF delivered at the Closed Session of the Second ASEM Leaders' Summit in London on 3 April 1998.*)

ASEF: Enhancing Mutual Understanding between Asia and Europe

Introduction

At the historic Asia–Europe Meeting (ASEM) held in Bangkok on 1 March 1996, the 26 leaders of Asia and Europe agreed to build a comprehensive partnership between the countries of the two regions and to promote peace and prosperity, based upon the principles of mutual benefit and mutual respect. The summit created only one institution, the Asia–Europe Foundation. The Foundation was mandated to enhance better mutual understanding between Asia and Europe through greater intellectual, cultural and people-to-people exchanges.

From Conception to Birth

Agreement to establish the foundation was achieved at the ASEM Senior Officials Meeting (SOM) in Dublin in December 1996. It was also agreed to incorporate the foundation, under the laws of Singapore, in accordance with the so-called Dublin Principles. The foundation was launched by the ASEM foreign ministers on 15 February 1997. The Board of Governors of the foundation held its first meeting on 17 February 1997 in Singapore.

Three Questions for ASEF

ASEF has been in existence for slightly over three years. What has it achieved? Has it proved its usefulness? What should be its future priorities and strategies?

ASEF's Philosophy

It is important to understand the ASEF philosophy because it governs our corporate culture and guides our actions. The ASEF philosophy is to be proactive and not reactive; to add value and to avoid duplicating what others are doing; to be bold and visionary; to work in partnership with other relevant and reputable organisations; to build networks with all sectors of society including the private sector and non-governmental organisations; to be cost-efficient and to avoid grandiose ideas; and to be supportive of the ASEM process and ASEM countries. Our ambition is for the **ASEF** brand name to stand for quality and intellectual rigour.

ASEF's Financial Muscle

The partners of ASEF have pledged a total of US$21.6 million to the Foundation. Of this amount, US$14.5 million have been paid up. So far, ASEF has spent S$7.1 million, leaving S$15.5 million in the balance.

What Has ASEF Achieved?

First, ASEF has implemented 52 projects involving over 3,000 participants. In accordance with ASEF's objective of giving every country a sense of ownership of the Foundation, the projects were held in 18 different countries.

ASEF's Role as Interpreter between Asia and Europe

Second, Asians and Europeans are often not fully aware of or understand the important developments which take place in the two regions. The birth of the euro was one such example. ASEF has organised three European Monetary Union roadshows in Hong Kong, Singapore and China. The East Asian monetary and economic crisis was another example. ASEF co-organised, with a French think-tank, a conference in Paris to discuss the crisis. The historic election in Indonesia, in June 1999, was a third example. ASEF co-organised, with the British Council, a preview of the election for the benefit of journalists from the two regions.

ASEF's Role as Intellectual Entrepreneur

Third, in order to increase mutual understanding, ASEF has organised or co-organised a series of important conferences, colloquia, meetings and lectures. The purposes of such activities are to build networks and to increase points of convergence and reduce points of divergence. The participants range from established leaders to scholars, journalists, businessmen and women, representatives of international organisations and non-governmental organisations, teachers and students. The topics discussed covered a broad spectrum, including the nexus between economic management and good governance, labour standards and international trade, human rights and human responsibilities, Myanmar, Asian and European values, the rights of minorities, and the launching of a new WTO round of multilateral trade negotiations.

ASEF as Cultural Impresario

Fourth, Asia and Europe are blessed with many rich and vibrant cultures. ASEF has tried to play a role in bringing the cultures of the two regions to each other, to build new networks of Asian and European artists, and to encourage collaboration between them. ASEF has co-sponsored a cultural forum in Paris, various arts events in London at the time of ASEM II, a meeting of publishers, film festivals, a workshop and a conference on the conservation of heritage, training of cultural managers, cultural and education television, and cultural and creative industries. ASEF is currently working closely with Korea on a number of cultural events which will be held in Korea at or around the time of ASEM III.

Investing in the Leaders of Tomorrow

Fifth, in line with our leaders' request, ASEF has invested considerable resource and attention on the young. We have used the Internet to link high schools in Asia and Europe. We ran an annual summer school for some of the brightest university students from the two regions. We held a very successful retreat for young parliamentarians, which was repeated in Lisbon recently. We have held a very productive forum for young entrepreneurs in Berlin. We have launched new initiatives involving interns and young forestry officials. In accordance with the mandate given to us by ASEM SOM, we convened a meeting in November 1999, at INSEAD in Fontainebleau, to brainstorm on the Asia–Europe Education Hub Proposal. The meeting was very successful. It was attended by representatives of about 60 universities. They have agreed to participate in the ASEM Education and Research Network or EARN.

ASEF's Role as a Clearing House

Sixth, ASEF has tried to play the role of a clearing house. ASEF has developed the most comprehensive inventory of all ASEM activities. It is called "An ASEM Companion", located on our website and is regularly updated. ASEF has also completed an inventory of the existing intellectual exchanges between the two regions. This is also available on our website. We have also established links between our website and other relevant sites of ASEM members. Our website receives an average of 10,000 visits a month.

Towards the Future

At 3½ years old, ASEF is still an infant. It has, however, been a precocious child. It has already accomplished much. There is, however, much more to be done. Looking to the future, ASEF intends to focus on the following four priorities: (i) education and youth; (ii) economic, political and security dialogue; (iii) culture and the arts; and (iv) media and communications. We believe that the partnership between East Asia and Western Europe will endure and prosper. ASEF's mission is to help anchor this partnership in the hearts and minds of the peoples of the two regions. ASEF intends to submit a report card to ASEM's leaders at their third summit in Seoul in October 2000. If our leaders are pleased with our report card we hope they will address the question of how to put ASEF on a sound financial standing for the long term.

(Report by ASEF to ASEM Senior Officials Meeting — period covered from 15 February 1997 to 15 March 2000.)

The ASEF Story
The First Three Years

PM Goh's Vision

The historic summit in Bangkok, between the sixteen leaders of the European Union and ten leaders of East Asia, held on 1 March 1996, was the realisation of Singapore Prime Minister Goh Chok Tong's vision. In September 1994 in Singapore, and subsequently at Davos in early 1995, Prime Minister Goh made the argument that the time had come for the European Union and East Asia to forge closer ties to complement their strong ties with the United States. At the Bangkok Summit, Prime Minister Goh made an interesting observation and proposal. He observed that the new and comprehensive partnership between Asia and Europe should not be confined to government and business. It should include the civil societies of the two regions. Towards this end, he proposed the establishment of the Asia–Europe Foundation (ASEF). He offered to host the Foundation in Singapore, to provide the Foundation with its first Executive Director, and to give it an initial grant of US$1 million. PM Goh's proposal was adopted by the summit (see Annex I for the text of the relevant paragraphs in the Chairman's Statement).

The Period of Gestation

In May 1996, I was asked by my government to agree to be nominated as the first Executive Director of the Asia–Europe Foundation. Although an Americanist rather than a Europeanist by background, I accepted the challenge of building bridges between East Asia and the European Union with enthusiasm.

The first concept paper on ASEF was written by Dr Lee Tsao Yuan of the Institute of Policy Studies. After several revisions, the paper was circulated to the 26 partners of the Asia Europe Meeting process (ASEM) in July 1996. The paper appears in Annex II.

Consultations on the concept paper were held bilaterally and multilaterally from May to October 1996. In order to accelerate the process of consultations and achieve a better understanding of the thinking in Europe, I was asked to undertake a trip to the major capitals of the European Union. Accompanied by Michelle Teo-Jacob, of the Ministry of Foreign Affairs, I visited Bonn, Brussels, London and Paris from 7 to 15 October 1996. In Brussels, I was disheartened to learn from my interlocutors in the European Commission that it would normally take two years to translate a vision into reality. I responded that I was determined to translate the vision of the Bangkok Summit into reality in eleven months. Why eleven months? Because the first ASEM Foreign Ministers' Meeting would be held in Singapore on 15 February 1997. Upon my return to Singapore, I revised the concept paper and wrote an explanatory note dated 17 October 1996. These appear in Annex III.

The Dublin Principles

I attended the ASEM Senior Officials Meeting (SOM) in Dublin on 19 and 20 December 1996. When the meeting started, there was still no agreement on the legal basis on which the Asia–Europe Foundation would be established. What was the sticking point? The sticking point was whether the Foundation would be incorporated as an international organisation, under an international legal agreement, or under Singapore's domestic law. The preference of the ASEAN partners, including Singapore, was for the first option. However, this was not acceptable to the European partners, Japan and Korea because of the legal complications of ratifying an international legal agreement under their respective constitutions.

I undertook a series of consultations on the margin of the SOM on 19 December. As a result of those consultations, consensus was achieved. The ASEM SOM adopted the Dublin Principles (Annex IV) on 20 December 1996.

Impressive Show of Support

Following the adoption of the Dublin Principles, every delegation took the floor to express its support for ASEF. Some delegations, namely, France, Singapore and the United Kingdom, pledged financial support as well as the secondment of staff. Other delegations pledged financial support. The spontaneous and generous expressions of support were a good omen for ASEF's future.

The Process of Incorporation

Upon my return from Dublin, and working closely with our first Company Secretary, Mr Foo Kim Boon, our first Singapore Governor, Dr Yeo Ning Hong, and my former Special Assistant, Ms Leigh Ann Pasqual, we succeeded in incorporating ASEF under Singapore's Company Act, as a company limited by guarantee. The Ministry of Finance agreed to confer on it the status of an institute of public character (IPC), thereby exempting it from tax. The Ministry of Foreign Affairs agreed to grant ASEF the same privileges and immunities as it had granted the APEC Secretariat. The Ministry of Communications and the Ministry of Manpower also acceded to ASEF's requests for exemptions in respect of the cars purchased and domestic help employed by ASEF's non-Singaporean professional staff. The Singapore Government agreed to make available a historic colonial building, at No. 1 Nassim Hill, as the premises of the Foundation.

The Birth of ASEF

On 15 February 1997, Singapore hosted the first meeting of ASEM foreign ministers. In a special ministerial declaration (Annex V), the ministers welcomed the establishment of ASEF and renewed their commitment to ensuring its success. On that evening, a reception was held at the Foundation's premises. The plaque of the Foundation was unveiled by the Foreign Minister of Singapore, Professor S Jayakumar, and the Foreign Minister of the Netherlands, Mr Hans van Mierlo, representing the Presidency of the European Union, in the presence of their ministerial colleagues.

First Board Meeting

The first meeting of the Board of Governors was held on 17 February 1997. The meeting elected Dr Helmut Haussmann of Germany as its first Chairman and Ambassador Koji Watanabe of Japan as Vice-Chairman.

The Board appointed me as the Foundation's Executive Director and Mr Pierre Barroux as Deputy Executive Director for a period of three years, on secondment from our respective governments. The Board empowered us to form the management of the Foundation. It also approved the budget and the programme of work.

The Board also created an Executive Committee consisting of the Chairman, Vice-Chairman, the Governor of Singapore, the Executive Director and Deputy Executive Director.

Evolution of the Board and Governance

In order to give as many governors as possible an opportunity to serve as chairman and vice-chairman, the Board decided to limit their tenure to one year. In the second year, Ambassador Koji Watanabe served as Chairman and Mr Edmond Israel of Luxembourg as Vice-Chairman. In the third year, Mr Israel served as Chairman and Ambassador Jay-Hee Oh of Korea as Vice-Chairman.

The Board decided to meet twice a year, once in Asia and once in Europe. The frequency of the Board meetings serves two useful purposes. First, it accelerates the bonding of the governors as friends and colleagues. Second, it gives the different host countries a greater sense of ownership of the Foundation. The Board has met in Singapore, Luxembourg, Bangkok, The Hague, Beijing, Copenhagen and Vienna. The management has also tried to organise projects alongside each Board meeting to give the Board more opportunities to take part in the work of the Foundation.

The third Chairman, Mr Edmond Israel, made three important contributions to the Board's governance. With the consent of the Board, he expanded the membership of the Executive Committee to include the two immediate former chairmen, and created an Audit Committee and a Nominating Committee.

ASEF's Management

Pierre Barroux and I gradually built up our management team. We urged governments of ASEM members to second personnel to the management, again to encourage their sense of ownership of the Foundation. The Director for Intellectual Exchange, Mr Duncan Jackman, was seconded by the British Government. He joined the team in August 1997. The Director for People-to-People Exchange, Mr Ulrich Niemann, was seconded by the German Government. He joined the team in August 1997. The Director for Cultural Exchange, Mr Cai Rongsheng, was seconded by the Chinese Government. He joined the team in September 1998. The Director for Public Affairs, Ms Peggy Kek, joined ASEF in June 1997. The Director for Administration and Finance, Mr Terence Tan, joined ASEF in April 1998, succeeding Ms Lee Geok Lian. Ms Leigh Ann Pasqual, the Special Assistant to the Executive Director, joined ASEF on 17 February 1997 and left on 10 December 1999. Ms Sharon Ong joined ASEF in April 1997, initially as a Special Assistant for Projects and now works as a Project Manager in Intellectual

Exchange. Mr Andreas Sieren is a Project Manager in People-to-People Exchange. Ms Amelia Lim is a Project Manager in Public Affairs. As a matter of policy and preference, the management team has always been small. It is a relatively flat organisation with no bureaucracy.

No organisation can work effectively without a good team of supporting staff. This is true of ASEF. The Executive Director and Deputy Executive Director are supported by Jenny Tan, Maggie Ramalingam, Christine Sipiere and Satwant Kaur. The Director of Intellectual Exchange is supported by Betty Ng and Geraldine Ang. The Director for People-to-People Exchange is supported by Angeline Toh and an intern, Carolyne Byrne. The Director of Cultural Exchange is supported by Wendy Lee and Marie Le Sourd. The Director of Public Affairs is supported by Tia Siew Keng and Yap Su-Yin. Finally, the Director of Administration is supported by Jenny Fong. The Foundation's two drivers are Mr S Vetrivelu and Mr Basri bin Borhan.

ASEF's Mission

The mission of ASEF is enshrined in the Chairman's Statement at the Bangkok Summit. It is to enhance better mutual understanding between Asia and Europe. How would this be achieved? Through greater intellectual, cultural and people-to-people exchanges. In addition to those three sectors we have added public affairs. Why? Because it is not enough for the Foundation to do good work. We have to let the world know about it. Also, the mass media is another constituency that we wish to cultivate. The Foundation, therefore, has four constituencies in the two regions: intellectuals, cultural leaders, talented and outstanding young people and members of the media.

ASEF's Agenda

What is ASEF's agenda? The first agenda item is to create networks in the four sectors which did not exist earlier. Towards this end, we have brought together, for example, high schools in the two regions through the use of the Internet; university students at our summer schools; young parliamentarians; editors and journalists; scholars, think-tankers and universities; painters, musicians, playwrights, arts managers, publishers and other representatives of cultural industries; and high officials and other policy-makers. ASEF has gone a long way towards fulfilling its first agenda item of networking.

Interpreter

The second item on the agenda of ASEF is to interpret important developments taking place in one region to the people of the other region. Let me cite a few examples. When East Asia was first hit by a monetary and economic crisis in 1997, there was very little understanding in Europe of the underlying causes of the crisis. Much of the analysis and commentary in the popular press in Europe was distorted by stereotypes and generalisations. ASEF co-organised a meeting in Paris with a French think-tank, CEPII, to forge a better understanding of the crisis.

The European Monetary Union (EMU) is a monumental achievement. The birth of the "euro" has transformed Europe and it will have a major impact on the world. Unfortunately, there is very little understanding of the EMU and the euro in Asia. In order to rectify this situation, ASEF has held three EMU roadshows, in Hong Kong, Singapore and Beijing.

Convergence and Divergence

The third agenda item of ASEF is to increase the points of convergence and reduce the points of divergence between the thinkers of the two regions. Towards this end, ASEF has organised or co-organised conferences, colloquia, seminars and workshops on important and controversial topics, such as human rights and values; whether trade should be linked to core labour standards and social conditions; the question of Myanmar; good governance and good economic management; and issues relating to the proposal to launch a new round of World Trade Organisation (WTO) negotiations.

Flagship Projects

It is often said that a good organisation should have one or more flagship projects. Does ASEF have any flagship projects? I would identify a few. First, the ongoing series of Asia–Europe Lectures. Our first three lecturers were the former president of the European Commission, Jacques Santer; the former prime minister of Thailand, Anand Panyarachun; and the current prime minister of Luxembourg, Jean-Claude Juncker.

Second, the annual Europe–Asia Forum which brings together about 50 high-level officials and business and civil society leaders. The forum is co-organised with the Herbert Quandt Stiftung of Germany, and the Institute of Policy Studies of Singapore.

Third, the annual ASEF Summer School for university students. This brings together some of the brightest students of the two regions for two weeks of living, learning and networking.

Fourth, the ASEF Young Parliamentarians' Meeting. This is a unique forum which brings together parliamentarians below the age of 40. The first two meetings, held in the Philippines and Portugal, were highly successful. It is now an annual event.

Fifth, the ASEF Editors' Roundtable. The first roundtable took place in Luxembourg in October 1997. The journalists were asked to comment on the results of a research, commissioned by ASEF, on how the print media of each region was reporting on the other. The second ASEF Editors' Roundtable will take place in Seoul at the time of ASEM III in October 2000 to look at "The Media's Impact on Public Opinion and Foreign Policy". In October 1998, the Colloquium for Journalists was held in Singapore, on the margin of the World Economic Forum's East Asia Economic Summit, on "How Europe Can Help East Asia without Provoking a Backlash". In June 1998, ASEF brought together in Jakarta, Indonesia, a group of Asian and European journalists to preview the historic elections in Indonesia.

Sixth, ASEF has put on its website the most comprehensive inventory of ASEM activities. It is called "An ASEM Companion" and is updated regularly. "An ASEM Companion" provides summaries of meetings convened by ministers and senior officials in fields such as trade, economics and foreign affairs. It also provides links to all the official ASEM websites.

Landmark Projects

ASEF has held some landmark events, which have led to other projects. The Cultural Forum, held in Paris in February 1998, was one such event. The forum was not only attended by an impressive cast of participants, but it also resulted in seven deliverables. Another highly successful event was the conference held at INSEAD, in Fontainebleau, France, to brainstorm on the Asia–Europe Education Hub proposal. The meeting was attended by some of the best universities from the two regions. The meeting agreed to proceed to launch the education hub project. Almost 200 new scholarships were offered by the participating universities. The third example was the conference on education in a knowledge-based economy, held in Luxembourg in May 2000. This conference was conceptualised as the first of a series of conferences inspired by the overarching theme of "New Thinking for a New Millennium".

ASEF's Philosophy

From the outset, ASEF decided not to function like a traditional, grant-giving Foundation. Instead, it preferred to be proactive in setting its own agenda. It preferred to use its limited funds to seed its agenda and to be actively involved in conceptualising and implementing its projects. This decision disappointed the research community, which had hoped that ASEF would function like a traditional grant-giving foundation.

ASEF's philosophy is to be proactive and not exclusive. On the contrary, its preference is to be inclusive. Therefore, for almost all of its projects, it has looked for partners in the host country and elsewhere. As a result, ASEF has developed an extensive network of partners with which it has co-organised projects. In addition, it has been very successful in finding co-sponsors from the private sector. This is important not just financially but because we believe that, in our new world, we should encourage the government, business and civil societies to work together in a spirit of tripartitism.

Part of ASEF's philosophy is to avoid duplicating what has been done before. We will not undertake a project unless it adds value. We will not accept any proposal unless it satisfies our twin criteria of relevance and coherence. We will usually not undertake an initiative unless it has at least a deliverable. Finally, we will decline a request if we feel that it is in an area which ASEF has no comparative advantage.

Conclusion

In the first three years of ASEF's life, it has implemented 55 projects in 18 of our 25 partner-countries. We have an alumni of 3,000. As the leader of the first management team, I look back on our first three years with pride and satisfaction. We have succeeded in building many new bridges of understanding and friendship between our two civil societies. We have also strengthened many existing bridges. In a modest way, I believe that we have enhanced mutual understanding between Asia and Europe. The first team is preparing to pass the baton to the second team. We wish our successors good luck and success in this collective endeavour that is important not only to Asia and Europe but also to the rest of the world.

Annex I
Extracts from Chairman's Statement of the Asia–Europe Meeting, Bangkok, 2 March 1996

Promoting Cooperation in Other Areas

17. The Meeting called for the strengthening of cultural links between Asia and Europe, particularly the fostering of closer people-to-people contacts, which is indispensable to the promotion of greater awareness and understanding between the peoples of both regions. The Meeting emphasised that these new links between Asia and Europe should help overcome misconceptions that may exist between the two regions, and could be further reinforced through promoting cultural, artistic, educational activities and exchanges involving particularly youth and students, and tourism between the two sides. In this respect, the Meeting was informed about the results of the Europe–Asia Forum on culture, values and technology, recently held in Venice. The Meeting also encouraged cooperation in the preservation of cultural heritage.

Future Course of ASEM

The Meeting agreed to the following follow-up measures:

19. An Asia–Europe Foundation would be set up in Singapore with contributions from Asian and European countries, to promote exchanges between think-tanks, peoples and cultural groups. In this connection, Singapore has offered to contribute US$1 million to seed this foundation.

Annex II
The Asia–Europe Foundation (ASEF): A Concept Paper

Background

1. The inaugural Asia–Europe Leaders Meeting (ASEM) on 1–2 March 1996 agreed to the establishment of an Asia–Europe Foundation (ASEF). The ASEM Chairman's Statement recorded that: "The ASEF would be set up in Singapore with contributions from Asian and European countries, to promote exchanges between think-tanks, peoples and cultural groups. In this connection, Singapore will contribute US$1 million to seed the Foundation." (Para 19)

2. This paper describes the objectives, core activities, structure, financing and a suggested approach for the immediate launching of the ASEF.

Objectives

3. The mission of the ASEF will be to promote closer ties between Asia and Europe, by enhancing and strengthening mutual understanding and greater interaction between the peoples of Asia and Europe. The ASEF's objectives is to work towards a future where Asians and Europeans can interact and cooperate with each other with greater familiarity, knowledge, ease and comfort. In the 21st century, Asia and Europe's dealings with each other should be as natural, informed and as familiar as if we were neighbouring regions.

4. To this end, the ASEF will organise and support activities in the educational, intellectual, cultural, economic, security and

scientific fields, in order to increase understanding and facilitate networking between Asia and Europe. The ASEF is unique in its mission of linking the two regions, Asia and Europe, on a pan-regional basis, in contrast to the more traditional objectives of promoting bilateral linkages. Hence, the ASEF's coordinating role for all ASEM activities related to people-to-people exchanges is not designed to supplant or supersede the activities of existing organisations, but rather to be an information centre, facilitator and catalyst for these ASEM activities, and to assist the existing organisations when necessary.

Core Activities

5. The activities of the ASEF will, in the long term, cover a wide range of areas. However, in the initial years, the ASEF should concentrate on a few core activities. These include:
- Network of think-tanks and researching institutes;
- An annual conference of emerging young leaders;
- Student exchanges;
- Promotion of Asian studies in Europe and European studies in Asia;
- Research and promotion of academic and scientific exchanges; and
- Promotion of cultural events.

Network of think-tanks and research institutes

6. The ASEF will promote networking among think-tanks and research institutes in Asia and Europe, and providing grants for projects which will further greater understanding of the societies, cultures, economics and strategic thinking in the two regions.

Annual conference of emerging young leaders

7. The conference of emerging young leaders will bring together promising young individuals from the fields mentioned in paragraph 4 above, aged between 30 and 40, from the ASEM

countries (for example, two from every country). Held once a year, the venue could be rotated among the ASEM countries. The Conference should focus on topics such as Asian and European cultures, economic and security trends in Asia and Europe, etc. The topics should be relevant to the ASEM process and enhance Asia–Europe understanding.

Student exchanges

8. In order to foster an in-depth understanding of the peoples and cultures of Asia and Europe among the young, the ASEF will organise student exchanges among Asian and European universities, on a selected basis.

Promotion of Asian and European studies in Europe and Asia

9. The ASEF will also promote the establishment of Asian and European studies in Europe and Asia by working with relevant institutions in both regions.

Research and promotion of academic and scientific exchanges

10. Apart from conducting research and studies, the ASEF can facilitate exchanges of academics, scientists and researchers, which will also serve to foster better understanding and cooperation.

Promotion of cultural events

11. Cultural events, such as art and history exhibitions, concerts, stage and dance performance will also improve awareness between the peoples of Asia and Europe. In addition to intellectual activities, the ASEF will therefore also promote events in conjunction with future ASEM meetings.

12. The ASEF will organise one major function every year, which will be its flagship event. The inaugural event could be a conference of the heads of the major think-tanks in Asia and Europe, to be held in 1997.

13. With its headquarters in Singapore, the ASEF will cooperate closely with existing organisations in the ASEM countries which have similar objectives, and with prominent individuals who are committed to strengthening the ASEM process. The forms of cooperation could vary from country to country; the ASEF should adapt flexibly to local circumstances.

14. In addition to organising its own activities, the Foundation will also co-organise projects with existing institutions in ASEM countries, and facilitate events organised by such institutions which have the objectives of promoting greater understanding and cooperation between Asia and Europe.

Structure

15. The ASEF should be established as an independent non-profit organisation. The ASEF will have the legal capacity of a body corporate, and will be governed by Headquarters Agreement between Singapore and the ASEF. The ASEF will report to the Asia–Europe Leaders Meeting, through the ASEM Senior Officials.

16. The organisation of the ASEF will comprise:
- a Council of Governors;
- a Committee of Advisors; and
- a Director-General and other professional and administrative staff.

Council of Governors

17. The Council of Governors of the ASEF will provide the oversight and broad direction for the Foundation. The Council will also be responsible for the Foundation's policies, programmes, priorities, fund-raising and the approval of the annual budget.

18. The Council of Governors will:

- comprise representatives from each ASEM member who are appointed in their personal capacity;
- comprise individuals of international stature, such as former Heads of Government, prominent businessmen, well-respected academics, and heads of media organisations;
- reflect an even balance between Asians and Europeans from the ASEM countries;
- be appointed by the ASEM Leader's Meeting;
- serve a renewable term of four years; and
- meet at least once a year

19. The Chairman of the Council and the Director-General should alternate between a European and an Asian respectively. For example, if the Chairman is European, the Director-General should be Asian, and vice versa.

Committee of Advisors

20. The Committee of Advisors will provide expert advice on the programmes of the ASEF, such as the themes and speakers for the conferences, the structure of exchange programmes and the nature of cultural activities.

21. The Committee will:
- comprise ten individuals appointed in their personal capacity;
- comprise recognised experts in various fields such as international relations, sociology, religion, the sciences and economics;
- comprise nationals of the ASEM countries, reflecting an even balance between Asians and Europeans;
- be appointed by the Board of Governors; and
- serve a renewable term of four years.

Staff

22. The staff of the ASEF will be nationals of the ASEM countries. They will, on the initial phase, comprise:
- A Director-General;

- A Deputy Director-General;
- A Director of Corporate Services; and
- Administrative and support staff.

Programme Directors, each with specific portfolios such as youth exchange programmes; networks of think-tanks, etc., could be appointed at a later stage.

23. The Director-General will be appointed for a five-year term by the Council of Governors. The positions of Director-General and Deputy-Director-General should alternate between an Asian and a European respectively. For example, if the first Director-General is Asian, the Deputy Director-General will be European. The second Director-General should then be a European, with an Asian Deputy Director-General. The other professional positions of the ASEF will be recruited by the Director-General, in close consultation with the ASEM governments.

24. The professional staff of the ASEF will be granted privileges and immunities, similar to those granted to staff of international organisations based in Singapore, such as the APEC Secretariat.

Financing

25. The Governments of the ASEM countries will provide the primary source of funding. Funds could also be obtained from private sources such as business corporations, other foundations and individuals.

26. The Foundation will, in the initial years, require an annual operating budget of about US$5 million, the major portion of which will be in the form of grants from governments. It will also be desirable for the Foundation to establish from the outset an endowment fund.

27. In the first five years, the financial contributions to the Foundation will be on a voluntary basis. After this period, a formula for mandatory contributions by governments should

be implemented. The formula should reflect the capacity of each individual ASEM country to pay.

28. The ASEF should also encourage the principle of co-financing; that is, part of the project financing will be borne by the ASEF, and part by the co-organiser or host country.

29. The staff of the ASEF should not engage in fund-raising activities in the initial five years and should instead concentrate on the core activities of the ASEF. It is expected that the Board of Governors will have some responsibility for the Foundation's fund-raising.

30. The accounts of the ASEF will be supervised and approved by a Grants Committee, comprising members of the Council of Governors.

Suggested Approach for Immediate Launch of the ASEF

31. In order to expedite the launching of the ASEF so as to ensure that it is operationally functional well before the next ASEM Leaders' Meeting in the United Kingdom in the year 1998, it is proposed that the Singapore Government assume the responsibility for launching the ASEF by providing the following:

- A temporary Headquarters for the first five years of the functioning of ASEF, including the coverage of all the rental and renovation costs for the establishment of the office;
- A Singaporean of international stature to serve as the first Director-General of the ASEF, who will be assisted by a Principal Private Secretary; the other staff positions discussed in paragraph 22 will be filled by the Director-General in close consultation with all ASEM governments;
- A list of nominees for the Council of Governors and for the Committee of Advisors; this list should be initially endorsed at the meeting of ASEM Foreign Ministers in Singapore on 15 February 97 and subsequently approved by the ASEM Leaders' Meeting in the United Kingdom; and

- A commitment to provide an appropriate building to serve as the permanent Headquarters of the ASEF; all expenses for the establishment of this office will be met by the Singapore Government.

Annex III
Explanatory Note on the ASEF Concept Paper

1. Objective

1.1 The objective of ASEF is to promote intellectual, cultural, and people-to-people exchanges between Asia and Europe.

2. Means to Achieve the Objective

2.1 ASEF should avoid duplicating existing bilateral and multilateral exchanges between Asia and Europe in the three fields.

2.2 ASEF should attempt to add value by acting as a:
- clearing house;
- catalyst;
- facilitator; and
- organiser/convenor.

2.3 ASEF could, for example, provide grants to Asian and European institutions to implement a desired programme; bring Asian and European institutions together to collaborate on a desired programme; and, selectively, implement a few flagship projects of its own.

2.4 One possible flagship project is to organise or co-sponsor a Cultural Festival to coincide with the ASEM Leader's Meeting.

2.5 Another possible flagship project is to organise a sequel to the Conference of Asian and European intellectuals which was held in Venice in January 1996.

3. Funding for ASEF

3.1 Singapore has offered to contribute US$1 million to ASEF as seed money.

3.2 France and Luxembourg have announced that they will each contribute US$1 million. In the case of France, it has indicated that it will make a similar contribution on two or three occasions during the first five years.

3.3 Brunei, Thailand, Japan, Korea and Germany have indicated their willingness to make contributions.

3.4 During the first five years, contributions will be on a voluntary basis.

3.5 At the end of the fifth year, ASEM Governments will review the basis for funding ASEF, with a view to putting it on a sound financial footing.

3.6 ASEF will have an annual budget of about US$5 million.

3.7 ASEF will attempt to devote 80 per cent of its budget to programmes and 20 per cent to administration.

3.8 Any money received in excess of US$5 million per annum will be put in an endowment fund.

3.9 ASEF will establish an initial endowment fund of US$50 million. Singapore has approached the European Commission to donate US$25 million to the fund and has undertaken to raise the remaining US$25 million from Asia.

4. Structure of ASEF

4.1 Singapore's concept paper suggests a three-tier structure:
- a Board of Governors consisting of 26 members, one from each ASEM country plus one seat for the European Commission;
- an Advisory Committee consisting of 10 or more experts in the three fields of ASEF's core mandate; and
- the management

4.2 The Board should normally elect its own Chairman and Deputy Chairman. However, as an exceptional measure, the first Chairman and Deputy Chairman of the Board shall be recommended by the ASEM Foreign Ministers to the Board.

4.3 The Advisory Committee shall be appointed by the Board.

4.4 It is agreed that the management should be kept small. However, even a small management should include the Director, the Deputy Director, three programme officers, one office manager, an information officer, an accounts clerk, and the necessary complement of secretarial and clerical staff.

4.5 The Director and the Deputy Director should normally be appointed by the Board. However, as an exceptional measure in order to launch the ASEF expeditiously, the first Director and his deputy shall be recommended by the ASEM Foreign Ministers at their meeting in Singapore on 15 February 1997. Their appointments would have to be approved subsequently by the Board at its inaugural meeting.

4.6 Can we agree that the Director and its Deputy or Deputies should be seconded and paid for, in part or in full, by their respective governments during the first three years, while the rest of the staff, who must be nationals of the ASEM countries, should be recruited in the open market, on local terms, and paid for by the Foundation?

4.7 It seems to be generally agreed that the members of the Board, the Director and the Deputy Director should be appointed for a term of three years.

4.8 The ASEF is an international, non-profit organisation with international legal personality, appointed by and accountable to the ASEM Leaders through the ASEM Senior Officials.

5. Timing of ASEF's Launch

5.1 Singapore hopes that ASEF will be launched when the ASEM Foreign Ministers meet in Singapore in February 1997.

5.2 All the preparatory work for the launch of ASEF will be approved by ASEM Senior Officials at their meeting in Dublin, on 20 December 1996.

5.3 In order to launch ASEF, the ASEM Foreign Ministers will:

- sign a memorandum of understanding to establish ASEF;
- appoint the members of the Board of Governors and recommend them to the ASEM Leaders for their endorsement;
- recommend the first Chairman and Deputy Chairman to the Board in accordance with paragraph 4.2 above; and
- recommend the Director and the Deputy Director to the Board in accordance with paragraph 4.5 above.

5.4 The Board of Governors will hold its first meeting as soon as possible after the ASEM Foreign Ministers' Meeting.

17 October 1996

The Asia–Europe Foundation (ASEF)
A Concept Paper (Revised)

Background

1. The inaugural Asia–Europe Leaders Meeting (ASEM) on 1–2 March 1996 agreed to the establishment of an Asia–Europe Foundation (ASEF). The ASEM Chairman's Statement recorded that: "The ASEF would be set up in Singapore with contributions from Asian and European countries, to promote exchanges between think-tanks, peoples and cultural groups. In this connection, Singapore will contribute US$1 million to seed the Foundation." (paragraph 19)

2. This paper describes the objectives, core activities, structure, financing and a suggested approach for the immediate launching of the ASEF.

Objectives

3. The mission of the ASEF will be to promote closer ties between Asia and Europe, by enhancing and strengthening mutual understanding and greater interaction between the peoples of Asia and Europe. The ASEF's objective is to work towards a future where Asians and Europeans can interact and cooperate with each other with greater familiarity, knowledge, ease and comfort. In the 21st century, Asia and Europe's dealings with each other should be as natural, informed and as familiar as if we were neighbouring regions.

4. To this end, the ASEF will organise and support ASEM's activities involving people-to-people exchanges in the educational, intellectual, cultural, economic, security and scientific fields, in

order to increase understanding and facilitate networking between Asia and Europe. The ASEF is unique in its mission of linking the two regions, Asia and Europe, on a pan-regional basis, in contrast to the more traditional objectives of promoting bilateral linkages. Hence, the ASEF's role is not designed to supplant or supersede the activities of existing organisations, but rather to be an information centre, coordinator, facilitator and catalyst for these ASEM activities, and to assist the existing organisations when necessary.

Core Activities

5. The activities of the ASEF will, in the long term, cover a wide range of areas. However, in the initial years, the ASEF should concentrate on a few core activities. These could include:
(a) networks of think-tanks and research institutes;
(b) networks of and dialogues between emerging young leaders;
(c) student exchanges;
(d) promotion of Asian studies in Europe and European studies in Asia;
(e) promotion of academic and scientific exchanges; and
(f) promotion of cultural events.

Networks of think-tanks and research institutes

6. The ASEF will promote networking among think-tanks and research institutes in Asia and Europe, and provide grants for projects which will further greater understanding of the societies, cultures, economies and strategic thinking in the two regions.

Dialogue between emerging young leaders

7. An annual conference of emerging young leaders, bringing together promising young individuals from the fields mentioned in paragraph 4 above, aged between 30 and 40, from the ASEM countries (for example, two from every country) could be held. The venue could be rotated among the ASEM countries. The

conference could focus on topics such as Asian and European values and cultures; economic and security trends in Asia and Europe. The topics should be relevant to the ASEM process and enhance Asia–Europe understanding.

Student exchanges

8. In order to foster an in-depth understanding of the peoples and cultures of Asia and Europe among the young, the ASEF will organise student exchanges among Asian and European universities, on a selected basis.[a]

Promotion of Asian and European studies in Europe and Asia

9. The ASEF will also promote the establishment of Asian and European studies in Europe and Asia by working with relevant institutions in both regions.

Promotion of academic and scientific exchanges

10. The ASEF will facilitate exchanges of academics, scientists and researchers, which will also serve to foster better understanding and cooperation.

Promotion of cultural events

11. Cultural events, such as art and history exhibitions, concerts, stage and dance performances will also improve the awareness between the peoples of Asia and Europe. In addition to intellectual activities, the ASEF will therefore also promote cultural events. For example, the ASEF could facilitate the organisation of cultural events in conjunction with future ASEM meetings.

---

[a]An example of such a university exchange programme is the Erasmus Programme organised by the European Commission.

12. The ASEF will organise one major function every year, which will be its flagship event. The inaugural event could be a conference of the heads of the major think-tanks in Asia and Europe, to be held in 1997 as a sequel to the Venice Forum.

13. With its headquarters in Singapore, the ASEF will cooperate closely with existing organisations in the ASEM countries which have similar objectives, and with prominent individuals who are committed to strengthening the ASEM process. The forms of cooperation could vary from country to country; the ASEF should adapt flexibly to local circumstances.

14. In addition to organising its own activities, the Foundation will also co-organise projects with existing institutions in ASEM countries, and facilitate events organised by such institutions which have the objective of promoting greater understanding and cooperation between Asia and Europe. ASEF could provide grants to such institutions.

Structure

15. The ASEF should be established as an international non-profit organisation. The ASEF will have the legal capacity of a body corporate, and will be governed by a Headquarters Agreement between Singapore and the ASEF. The ASEF will report to the Asia–Europe Leaders Meeting, through the ASEM Senior Officials.

16. The organisation of the ASEF will comprise:
(a) a Board of Governors;
(b) a Committee of Advisors; and
(c) a Director, a Deputy Director, and other professional and administrative staff.

Board of Governors

17. The Board of Governors of the ASEF will provide the oversight and broad direction for the Foundation. The Board will

also be responsible for the Foundation's policies, programmes, priorities, fund-raising and the approval of the annual budget.

18. The Board of Governors will:

- comprise representatives, one from each ASEM member, who are appointed in their personal capacity and a representative of the European Commission;
- comprise individuals of international stature, such as former high-ranking government officials, prominent businessmen, well-respected scholars and leading members of the mass media;
- be appointed by the ASEM Leaders, on the recommendation of the Foreign Ministers;
- serve a renewable term of three years; and
- meet at least once a year.

19. The Chairman of the Board and the Director should alternate between a European and an Asian respectively. For example, if the Chairman is European, the Director should be Asian, and vice versa.

Committee of Advisors

20. The Board of Governors may appoint a Committee of Advisors to assist the management in carrying out its mandate.

21. The Committee will
- comprise individuals appointed in their personal capacity;
- comprise recognised experts in the various fields relevant to the mandate of the Foundation;
- comprise nationals of the ASEM countries and reflect a balance between Asians and Europeans; and
- serve a renewable term of three years.

Management

22. The staff of the ASEF will be nationals of the ASEM countries. They will, in the initial phase, comprise:

- a Director;
- a Deputy Director;
- other professional staff; and
- administrative and support staff.

23. Programme Directors, each with specific portfolios such as intellectual exchange, cultural exchange, and people-to-people exchange, would be appointed at an appropriate time.

24. The Director will be appointed for a three-year term by the Board of Governors. The positions of Director and Deputy Director should alternate between an Asian and a European respectively. For example, if the first Director is Asian, the Deputy Director will be European. The second Director should then be a European, with an Asian Deputy Director. The other professional positions of the ASEF will be recruited by the Director, in the open market.

25. The professional staff of the ASEF will be granted privileges and immunities in accordance with the Headquarters Agreement between the Singapore Government and ASEF. They will be similar to those granted to staff of international organisations based in Singapore, such as the APEC Secretariat.

Financing

26. The governments of the ASEM countries will provide the primary source of funding. Funds could also be obtained from private sources such as business corporations, other foundations and individuals.

27. The Foundation will, in the initial years, require an annual operating budget of about US$5 million, the major portion of which will be in the form of grants from governments.[b] It will also be desirable for the Foundation to establish from the outset an endowment fund.

---

[b] The current budget of the Commonwealth Foundation is 2 million pounds sterling. 80 per cent of its budget is spent on programme activities and 20 per cent on administration.

28. In the first five years, the financial contributions to the Foundation will be on a voluntary basis. At the end of the fifth year, the ASEM governments will review the basis for funding ASEF, with a view to putting it on a secure financial footing.

29. The ASEF should also encourage the principle of co-financing, that is, part of the project financing will be borne by the ASEF, and part by the co-organiser or host country.

30. The staff of the ASEF should not engage in fund-raising activities and should instead concentrate on the core activities of the ASEF. It is expected that the Board of Governors will have some responsibility for the Foundation's fund-raising.

31. The accounts of the ASEF will be supervised and approved by a Finance Committee, comprising members of the Board of Governors.

Suggested Approach for Immediate Launching of the ASEF

32. In order to expedite the launching of the ASEF so as to ensure that it is operationally functional well before the next ASEM Leaders' Meeting in the United Kingdom in the year 1998, it is proposed that the Singapore Government assume the responsibility for launching the ASEF by providing the following:

(a) a temporary Headquarters for the first five years of the functioning of the ASEF, including the coverage of all the rental and renovation costs for the establishment of the office;

(b) a Singaporean of international stature to serve as the first Director of the ASEF, who will be assisted by a Principal Private Secretary; the other staff positions discussed in paragraph 22 will be filled by the Director in accordance with paragraph 24 above;

(c) a list of nominees for the Board of Governors; this list should be initially endorsed at the meeting of ASEM Foreign Ministers in Singapore on 15 February 1997 and subsequently approved by the ASEM Leaders' Meeting in the United Kingdom; and

(d) a commitment to provide an appropriate building to serve as the permanent Headquarters of the ASEF; all expenses for the establishment of this office will be met by the Singapore Government.

33. The first meeting of the Board of Governors or Directors will be held at the earliest possible time after the ASEM Foreign Ministers' Meeting on 15 February 1997.

Revised on 17 October 1996

Annex IV
Dublin Agreed Principles of the Asia–Europe Foundation

Purpose, Areas of Interest and Functions

1. The purpose of the Foundation is to promote better mutual understanding between Asia and Europe through greater intellectual, cultural and people-to-people exchanges, in line with the vision for Asia–Europe cooperation as laid down by the ASEM Leaders at their meeting in Bangkok from 1 to 2 March 1996.

2. In pursuit of this purpose, the Foundation should seek to add value by:
- giving grants;
- acting as a clearing house, catalyst and facilitator;
- collaborating with relevant Asian and European institutions of the ASEM countries;
- organising a few flagship projects of its own; and
- implementing any project assigned by future meetings of ASEM Leaders or Ministers and the relevant members of the European Commission.

3. The Foundation should avoid duplicating existing and future bilateral and multilateral exchanges between Asia and Europe in the three core areas of its work, as stated in paragraph 1 above, and should seek where possible to build on and promote further development in the activities of existing networks in these areas.

Participation

4. Participation in the Foundation shall be open to ASEM partners having taken part in the first ASEM in Bangkok in March 1996, as well as to any new partner joining the ASEM process.

5. Intellectual, cultural and other relevant institutions and non-governmental organisations of the ASEM partners, working in the three core areas of the Foundation's mandate, will be eligible to apply to the Foundation for assistance.

Funding for the Foundation

6. The Foundation will establish an operating fund and an endowment fund.

7. The Foundation shall be entitled to solicit and accept contributions for either of these funds from member governments and their institutions, as well as from private corporations, foundations or individuals.

8. Contributions will be on a voluntary basis. During the fifth year, ASEM governments and the European Commission will review the basis for funding the Foundation in future years.

9. Any moneys received in the operating fund in excess of the annual budget of the Foundation shall be transferred to the Endowment fund, which shall also receive any contributions specifically earmarked for this purpose.

Legal Capacity

10. The Foundation shall be incorporated under Singapore's domestic law as a not-for-profit corporation with tax exempt status. It will have the legal capacity to contract, acquire and dispose of movable and immovable property, and be party to legal proceedings.

Governance

11. The Foundation will be governed by a Board of Governors. Each participant will designate one Governor for a period of three years. The Board will meet at least once a year and more often, if necessary. The Board will, at its first meeting, formally adopt a statement of the Foundation's purpose, objectives and procedures. The Board will likewise draw up its own rules of procedure. It may appoint an Advisory Committee and any other committee as may, in its view, be necessary for the Foundation's functions.

12. The Board of Governors shall elect its own Chairman and Deputy Chairman for a period of one year. If the Chairman is a European, the Deputy Chairman shall be an Asian, and vice versa. The first Chairman and Deputy Chairman shall be elected by the Board at its first meeting, on the basis of nominations made at the ASEM Foreign Ministers' Meeting on 15 February 1997.

13. The Board of Governors will be responsible for determining the Foundation's policies, programmes and priorities. The Board of Governors shall also be responsible for ensuring the efficient use of the Foundation's resources, for the approval of the Foundation's annual report, its proposed budget and workplan for the coming year, and for transmitting annual reports of its finance and activities to participants. In the exercise of their responsibilities, members of the Board will have regard to the interest of the ASEM as a whole.

Staffing

14. The staff of the Foundation shall be headed by a Director. The Director will be a citizen of an ASEM country. He shall be appointed by the Board of Governors for a term of three years. The Director will be responsible to the Board for the administration of the Foundation and the implementation of its policies and programmes. The Foundation will be represented by the Director.

15. The Director will be assisted by a Deputy Director who will be a citizen of an ASEM country, appointed by the Board for a term of three years.

16. If the Director is an Asian, the Deputy Director will be a European, and vice versa. The first Director and Deputy Director shall be appointed by the Board of Governors at their first meeting on the basis of nominations received at the ASEM Foreign Ministers' Meeting on 15 February 1997.

17. The Director will recruit such professional, secretariat and other staff as are from time to time considered necessary for carrying out the policies and programmes of the Foundation. The Director will also seek the secondment of such staff where appropriate.

Accounts

18. The accounts of the Foundation shall be maintained according to normal principles of good practice, and shall be audited by an external auditor appointed by the Board whose reports shall be submitted to the Board.

19 December 1996

Annex V
Extract from Chairman's Statement at the First ASEM Foreign Ministers' Meeting, Singapore, 15 February 1997

The Ministers adopted a Declaration to welcome the establishment of the Asia–Europe Foundation (ASEF) in Singapore and they participated in the launching of the Foundation. Many ASEM partners pledged their contributions to the ASEF. They noted that the inaugural meeting of the ASEF Board of Governors would be held on 17 February 1997 in Singapore.

FOREIGN MINISTERS' MEETING
14–15 February 1997, SINGAPORE

The Asia–Europe Foundation Ministerial Declaration

We, the ASEM Foreign Ministers and the Vice-President of the European Commission,

Recalling that the Asia–Europe Foundation was approved by the Asia–Europe Meeting (ASEM) on 1 and 2 March 1996 in Bangkok, Thailand:

Noting that the ASEM Chairman's Statement, in paragraph 19, recorded:

"The Asia–Europe Foundation would be set up in Singapore with contributions from Asian and European countries, to promote exchanges between think-tanks, peoples and cultural groups."

Welcome the establishment of the Asia–Europe Foundation in Singapore and renew our commitment to ensure its success.

Request the 1998 Asia–Europe Meeting to review the status of the Foundation.

15 February 1997

About the Editors

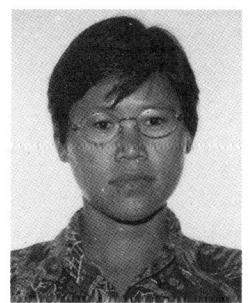

Yeo Lay Hwee, a Research Fellow in the Singapore Institute of International Affairs, focuses her research on Asia–Europe relations in general, and the ASEM process in particular. Her articles on Asia–Europe relations have appeared in various publications including *Southeast Asian Affairs 1997*; *ASIEN*; *Panorama*; and *Journal on Contemporary Southeast Asian Affairs*.

Asad Latif is a Senior Writer with *The Straits Times*, Singapore. He read English Honours at Presidency College, Calcutta, and later won the Raffles (Chevening) and S Rajaratnam scholarships to Cambridge, where he received his Master of Letters (M.Litt.) degree in History. Among his publications are a book *The Flogging of Singapore: The Michael Fay Affair*, which he wrote; and another book, *Walking the Tightrope: Press Freedom and Professionalism*, which he edited. He is married with a son.